The Last Best West

Women on the Alberta Frontier
1880–1930

ELIANE LESLAU SILVERMAN

FIFTH
HOUSE
PUBLISHERS

Front cover image courtesy Glenbow Archives, Calgary, Canada / NA-206-27
Back cover image courtesy Glenbow Archives, Calgary, Canada / NC-43-13
Hand coloring by Laurel Wolanski
Cover and interior design by Rachel Hershfield/RH Design
The publisher gratefully acknowledges the support of The Canada Council for the Arts and the Department of Canadian Heritage for our publishing program.

THE CANADA COUNCIL | LE CONSEIL DES ARTS
FOR THE ARTS | DU CANADA
SINCE 1957 | DEPUIS 1957

We acknowledge the financial support of the Government of Canada through the Book Publishing Industry Development Program for our publishing activities.

Printed in Canada.

98 99 00 01 02 / 5 4 3 2 1

CANADIAN CATALOGUING IN PUBLICATION DATA

Silverman, Eliane Leslau, 1939–
The last best West

ISBN 1-894004-15-9

1. Women immigrants—Alberta—History. 2. Women immigrants—Alberta—Social conditions. 3. Frontier and pioneer life—Alberta. I. Title.
HQ1459.A4S55 1998   305.4'097123'09041   C98-910745-0

Fifth House Ltd.
#9 - 6125 11 St. SE
Calgary, AB, Canada
T2H 2L6
1-800-360-8826

CONTENTS

INTRODUCTION

Thoughts and memories come together in a moment. Language and listening weave individual meaning with shared knowledge. Like a ball of yarn to be untangled, rolled up again, then reworked, words make memories the texture of our present as speakers breathe words to create a fabric of past and present, silky and rough. The past is not merely memory; it is omnipresent. The women who speak on the following pages offer us today, our own moment. "I remember," they say, and they help us to know our own meanings.

So I recall the origins of this book. I moved to Canada in 1967, to Calgary. The landscape, human and geographic, was new to me; far from any ocean, it was an almost somnolent city of fewer people than any city I had known, surrounded by flat farms and small towns whose purposes were unclear to me. During my first winter here, I drove often through the brown-sugar streets of the city and out into the prairie where tilled soil awaited its new season, and where roads engulfed one in isolation; a prairie of long gray or gold horizons lifting toward a sky that was alternately lifeless or white and cerulean. I stopped, walked, and listened in the January stillness. The historian in me asked what it felt like for the people who had arrived here before me. Why had they chosen this frontier? Did it feel to them like the end of the road or the beginning of something better? Had they brought their cultural and psychological baggage with them, or had they shed it to enter the new country? Did they view their lives through a lens of past experience and present reality combined? What had they expected? In fact, did they have expectations, or did they just come to this new frontier? What did they find? The woman in me wondered even more insistently about the women who settled here, as daughters, mothers, women on their own. What were their lives like? How did they perceive their own experience?

A story I heard that year added urgency to my questions. A woman from Minnesota had migrated to Saskatchewan with her husband during the 1920s. She lived in a sod house on the open prairie, far from any neighbors or trees, surrounded in winter only by snow and wind and sky. The roaring that she heard day and night, unmarked by the sight of movement (for there was nothing but her mind to be windblown), impelled her to plant a stick in the ground with a bright red handkerchief tied to it. When the rush of wind intensified, she could glance at the dancing red cloth for reassurance that the wind indeed blew and that she had not invented that lonely scream.

I was haunted by the poignancy of that story. But I knew that there must be other kinds of lives, a variety of stories that were surely as complicated and conflicting as those of women's lives today. Myths about frontier women, stories of heroism, self-sacrifice, and martyrdom would not suffice to explain the red handkerchief and hundreds of other tales. The myths elevated women to superhuman size, but they also reduced them to a uniformity, a sameness of experience. In time I realized that the way to understand women's lives was to hear women tell about them. As frontier women had not left many written documents that might convey their perception of their experience, I decided that I would simply talk to them.

Many women of that first generation of settlers were still living, in 1976, when I began interviewing women throughout Alberta. White settlers had begun arriving at this "last best west" in the mid-1880s, so it made sense to talk with as many women as possible who had come that early. When I began this work, it was still possible to do so. Even some of the earliest settlers were still living. I wanted to speak with women who had themselves made the migration, not with their daughters or granddaughters, for though family lore is surely part of what makes a culture, first-person accounts were what I needed to hear.

The next year took me all over the province. Some of the interviews took place in Calgary, others meant a short jaunt by car out of the city. Greater distances or snowy roads sometimes required visits, often by air, of several days or weeks in order to reach people in far-flung hamlets or on distant homesteads. I met women who were willing to share parts of their lives with me, recounting incidents, reliving feelings, and invariably welcoming me. That year was filled with good conversation and is alive in me still. Thoughts tumble—of cookies offered in small nursing-home rooms; of framed photographs proudly displayed, grandchildren resembling older, yellowed photos pulled from cardboard boxes; crocheted doilies; and once, a blue knit cap to take away with me. Tea or coffee was poured from elegant silver teapots set down by ornate flower arrangements, or from chubby brown pottery and accompanied by finely textured breads. More often, cups of instant coffee stood on the table between us. There were invitations to stay on for dinner, or to spend the night—and I often did, thus sharing present as well as past over dinner tables and on porches. There were offers of rides through unfamiliar countryside to reach neighbors and friends who quickly ceased to be strangers. Then there were

Leaving Montana, 1890.

repeated invitations to return, the warm good wishes repeated, too. Above all, of course, there was the readiness of people to share the details of their lives. The memories of the past flowed on, enhancing the present. The women, allowing me into their lives and their narratives, gave us a gift of themselves, and gave themselves a gift also; they restored themselves into our history.

The women who spoke with me, although initially reluctant, were eager, in the end, to tell their stories—eager, I think, to participate in the creation of a world in which women have a place, a place they would make public and visible. They were seeking historical validation, a sense of continuity, a knowledge of community and of their role in the western prairie community. Instead of spiritual isolation, they were aware of asserting a tradition, a continuum with those who were there before and those who will come after. They wanted to leave a trace of themselves, not to disappear unnoted. They knew that what has been deemed the private realm—and that is most often the realm of women—is as meaningful and as real as the public world of "important people." The words they spoke are part of the long process of making women visible in our tradition.

Each of them had a different story to tell; each told it in her own way, some straightforwardly, almost dispassionately, others eloquently and at length. Talking was a way of breaking the silence of history and the ever-threatening loneliness of old age. Communication becomes an island of refuge. As physical limitations increase, as the nearness of death is accepted, the parts of a person geared to the future grow less compelling. The way is cleared for the return of the past, a past which we need, men or women, to be ourselves fully human, grounded in time and place.

The experience of frontier women, their own stories in their own words, had been largely undocumented when I began this book. I interviewed over one hundred and fifty women. They were not chosen to be "representative;" they represent only the huge variety of ethnic, religious, racial, national, and class backgrounds of western women. In talking with them, I never sought a "typical" story but asked them only about their own experiences of migration and frontier life. And yet, their stories, as they came together, became not just a random collection of stories, but a collective autobiography.

In the southern part of Alberta, I began by interviewing people known to me, or to friends, or to friends' grandmothers. They led me to other women, their friends, or their neighbors. In the rest of the province, the health units were helpful in supplying the names of first-generation frontier women. Again, when traveling to see those women, they might introduce me to "my great friend," whom I would then interview. Sometimes, as I drove throughout the province, I stopped in a village or a hamlet, stepped into the store or the post office, introduced myself and explained what I was doing, and was sometimes told that I must speak with "old Mrs. Turner, who's been here forever." The interviews grew in number; patterns began to emerge.

Collecting the oral histories for this book took a year. I did interviews with women in their own homes, for the most part, in the spaces where they felt most comfortable. Most were conducted in English, several in French, though a few were in Cree and in Ukrainian, with a translator present. I phoned first, explained my project, and then sent a letter providing more detail, explaining that I hoped to hear and understand their perceptions of the frontier experience. Almost invariably, their first response was that perhaps I should talk to their husbands, or that it was a pity that their husbands were no longer living. Both over the phone and at the interview, I usually found it necessary to assure the women that it was their lives and their feelings in which I was interested. Their hesitation about their historical value revealed and reflected the lesson that history is so often about men, and especially about men with power. I tried to convey my certainty that the female half of the population must be incorporated into what we know of the past, and that their lives, however they had been lived, must be understood and included in our history, to become part of our present.

I taped all the interviews, which were later transcribed to preserve the precise nuances of their talk. The tape recorder sometimes seemed an intruder, but by the time I had plugged it in, put tapes into it, and talked about how I too have a certain distrust of machinery, its presence was forgotten. Coffee was served and we began to talk. The interviews lasted between two and eight hours. They usually began with an open-ended question: "How did you feel upon arriving here?" This question opened the floodgates of memory, especially releasing the highly charged emotions accompanying the journey and the settling in.

Thereafter, the women proceeded to talk about the events and feelings of their lives, less in terms of dates, of the year something had happened, and more in terms of their places in each woman's own perception of her life cycle. That is to say, the women organized their experience not by dates of provincial or federal elections, nor by wars or floods, nor even by a harvest or the acquisition of another building on the land, but by the daily rhythms of their own lives, which might be similar winter and summer, punctuated by visits, the birth of a child, or the purchase of a new kitchen table or linoleum floor. Thus grew the organization of this book, through the themes struck by the women themselves. In the years I sought to document, women perceived their lives in the private realm, rarely fitting even their paid labor into a public context. It is up to us, now, to integrate the private world of women into a public space, providing women a place in our common world.

Not all the women, of course, offered the same degrees of intensity in their recollections. Some talked with verve and enthusiasm, others with resignation. They conversed, of course, in the ways that grew out of their own lives, and their own personalities. Hardly one of them sought to aggrandize her own role. To the contrary, they always began by disclaiming their importance. "My life has not been very important," they might say, or, "Really, you should talk with someone who knew more about what was going on in politics." When I convinced her that I simply wanted to hear about her own life, and that, of course, her life mattered, each person spoke in a voice true to herself. The emotions of the past were released into the present; if facts and dates were not always clear, feelings were. I hope that I have faithfully, in turn, conveyed each woman's own insights and inflections. I retained their own words in every instance, deleting only the extra words and phrases we use when we converse. I have, however, changed all the women's names in honor of the intimacy of their accounts; the ethnicity of their names has been preserved.

This book, then, is part of our world's desire to place women in the history of the frontier. We have come to recognize that to write only about frontiersmen's stories distorts the history of settlement. Women in this book will tell their own stories about their lives, their workplaces, their communities, and their families on their own terms, as they themselves understood them. They will tell their own stories about what the frontier experience meant to the first generation of women who participated in the settlement process of the western frontier.

The country to which they came was the site of the last land rush in North America, completing a process that had begun three centuries earlier.

Opportunities, both economic and psychological, were available in the harsh demanding country of prairie, mountain, and brush. Women began arriving in urban and rural areas by 1885. They came from the United States and from eastern Canada, from Germany, the Ukraine, Italy, Japan, and elsewhere. Economic opportunity, improved chances for their children, the decisions of husbands, rebellion against the confines of traditional societies, or the lure of the west drew them to Alberta, touted as a land of openness. It was a land of diversity, from wheat and cattle country in the prairies, to coal mining in the foothills and mountains, to the forestry of the Rocky Mountains, to small industry in the few cities, to the impenetrable brush and muskeg of the north. Despite its rigors, Alberta beckoned; its population grew from 78,000 in 1900 to 750,000 in 1929.

Some of the women arrived to face the new land with nothing but a suitcase and a feather quilt. Others arrived laden with a piano, books, silver, and lace tablecloths. Many of them imported an array of cultural baggage, while others self-consciously left behind the world from which they had come. Language, customs, and patterns of relationships and hierarchies might be treasured or abandoned, cherished or reviled. They came from diverse ethnic and social backgrounds. Few of them knew what they might find in the new society.

Immigrant woman in front of immigration cabin, Medicine Hat, prior to going to her homestead in New Holland, 1911.

What they found depended often on chance and accident, more often indeed than the western myth had led them to believe. The accident of place: whether the homestead chosen as a spot on the map lay on the dry side of the hill; whether the neighbors in the town mocked a foreign accent; whether the lumber camp could take on men that winter; or whether there was a school nearby. The accident of time: the price grain commanded that year; a boom in construction the next fall; the local school board's ability, ever uncertain, to pay its female teacher.

Frontier women's reactions to new circumstances were influenced by the cultures and the psychologies they brought with them, individually or in communities of migration. A European, arriving with less than nothing and sometimes remaining virtually penniless, might still feel at home surrounded by people from the old country, while an English-speaking woman from a middle-class Ontario family might feel bereft among farming neighbors, never feeling as if she were one of them and always yearning for the past. A woman's response to the new life might arise from a self-conscious attempt to accept it, or conversely, from an almost conscious awareness that she could not and would not adapt.

The migration they made toward the west completed the process of settling the land in the "last best west" that had begun in the seventeenth century. Generation after generation, eastern Canadian, American, and European people, singly, with kin, or as villages, pushed outward from settled areas toward the unknown. Some sought to escape from rigid requirements in their societies to find greater freedom for themselves. Economic need drove others, influenced by railroad and government propaganda that promised wealth and a second chance. They moved to small settlements, towns at the end of the railroad line, or ventured beyond to where no one had settled before. They brought with them whatever they could, whether just the furnishings for a small room or even just a few garments, or tools, farm implements, sewing machines. One can only be awed by the migrants' bravery and foolhardiness, fortified only with maps and rumor, in leaving the stability of a social structure for a west about which they knew so little.

Perhaps women and men of the late nineteenth century were psychologically prepared for change. Since early in the century, they had seen their fellows come and go, sometimes going very far indeed. They, or their mothers or grandmothers, had witnessed the changes we know as the

Industrial Revolution, a transformation from a local agrarian economy to a world that would culminate in the assembly line and mass distribution and consumption. Women's roles had been profoundly altered by economic, social, and technological transformations. Industrialization provided some of them paid labor in jobs that were called unskilled and were poorly paid. It brought them the double day: the long days of work in often terrible conditions, combined with the never-ending labor in the household, the child rearing, the emotional care of their families. Industrialization also offered the opportunity to work with other women. By the early twentieth century some of them would begin organizing into trade unions, speaking in a united voice in hope of improving workplaces with protective legislation. The physical details of their lives had been transformed too: by 1900 they could buy bread, ready-made clothes, or wringer washing machines. They could ride elevators; twenty years later they could travel in automobiles. In 1929 people in Canada, listening as their radios broadcast the news of a world-wide economic depression, recognized beyond a doubt that local economies were now part of the international ripples and tides that would pour over them.

Changes in the myths and images of women accompanied the economic transformation. Formerly, the spinning, weaving, sewing, soap- and candle-making, butchering, and baking by rural women had been essential for the sustenance of their families; their places in the economy were clear. As men turned from agriculture to industry and commerce, some of them became wealthy enough to remove their wives from producing for the domestic family economy. Married to men who could afford wives who did not work for pay or who did not produce household necessities, middle-class women began to lose economic meaning. Instead of producing the necessities of everyday life, they took on new roles, becoming the "angels of the hearth," the guardians of children, the sole creators of "home," supposed to be a refuge from the competitive and rapidly changing world of the west. They did the emotional work of their households. The divisions between the realms of women and men became sharper. Male children learned, if one is to believe the child-raising manuals, to be aggressive, competitive, and individualistic, while female children learned to be compassionate and nurturing. Men and women came to seem like different kinds of people. Women came to be "ladies."

In that myth of the lady lay the seeds of change that blossomed in the campaign to gain the vote for women. The Canadian women's suffrage movement derived part of its strength from the progress women had made in education. Girls were earning more high school diplomas than boys and, by the last quarter of the nineteenth century, were gaining admission to colleges and normal schools. Some women, and some men, began to reject the arguments of physicians and educators that women's brains and nervous systems were incapable of intellectual effort. In doing so, they also came to believe that their uniqueness as women could serve them politically. In agitating for the vote for women, many of them argued that women would help male politicians maintain the health of families. They would also, they argued, bring the caring and nurturing influence of their homes into the public world of politics.

Indeed, women early in the twentieth century involved themselves in public work that fit with their vision of themselves as caretakers of emotions. Temperance, child welfare, allowances for mothers, labor reform, educational reforms, raising health care standards—women did that work to make the world more homelike. In political work, they expressed their belief in the redemptive power of women. Even as they did, subversive changes were taking place in women's lives. One such change was the westward movement.

As women of many ethnic, racial, and religious backgrounds came west, they acted as forces both for retaining and for changing the mythologies about women as morally superior. Most of them probably attempted to maintain old customs, bound as they were to parents, children, and husbands by ties of love or fear or economic necessity. Old patterns of deference often persisted in churchgoing, child raising, sexual relations, and employment. The family circle continued to be seen as the most appropriate setting for women's activities. Yet docility and obedience did not always serve well, when all hands were needed to set traplines, clear brush, take in lodgers, or wait on customers. In the west, women were needed as economically productive people. In the face of the need to work for survival, if not prosperity, women could hardly hope for leisure and protection. The myth of the lady began to crumble, inappropriate where women must participate in creating a society. Women seized chances to do more than adorn hearth and home. Custom and laws changed to accommodate new realities. Women gained the vote in Alberta in 1916. In 1929 they were defined as legal persons by the Privy Council's decision in the

"Person's Case." Workplaces acknowledged that their participation was vital to the new economy. With literacy levels close to those of men, and healthier bodies and more energy, women were ready to step out of the confines of the family into the communal world.

They began to take halting steps toward autonomy and independence. They did so at first in the company of other women, in sewing circles, church auxiliaries, women's farm organizations, councils of women, Women's Institutes, and temperance unions. From those efforts they derived personal strength that would eventually lead them to political efforts on their own behalf. As they moved out of individual families into community, they provided the province with the institutions that would make it more than a collection of individuals—truly a culture.

Not that their paths were straight and true. Political gains could be followed by cultural losses. Women's early efforts to gain access to professional jobs were undermined in the twenties by college women who sought husbands as the goal of their education. The few women elected to the provincial legislature were not followed by growing numbers of women, nor usually by any female legislators at all. It would be years before women would agitate with much success for equal pay, professional work, or greater personal safety.

Yet the seeds for community were planted when women began arriving in Alberta. Torn from the familiar, they were forced to create something new. Some vanquished the unknown with tradition, albeit altered by the new environment. Others sought new understandings of a new place. Some remained isolated, glad or sad of it; some joined together as workers, citizens, mothers, and women. Responses were individual, and yet patterns emerged. Their stories so long neglected, women can now tell us what the frontier experience was like for them. We are the heirs of their narratives.

This is a set of stories, then, a collective autobiography about migration and adaptation. From the stories of the voyage westward, the voices diverge and recombine to weave subtle patterns, giving texture to our own lives today. The voices share strengths, doubts, thoughts and feelings, adventures and experiences, reaching out of isolation to become our own history, our common world.

MIGRATION

T he first experience shared by western Canadian women was the migration they made. They came from eastern Canada to Alberta by train most often; the shorter jaunts from south of the Canadian border were made by wagon, or later, by automobile. From Europe, of course, they came by ship, first traveling overland to a port city where they crowded into boats for the ocean crossing, and then across the continent "on the steel." The journey was invariably long. Its physical discomforts were intensified by a yearning for what lay irrevocably behind and an apprehension of the unknown that lay ahead.

Uprooted from one culture and set down in a new geography that was not even a culture yet but just a place in the making—a frontier—Alberta's women were all travelers, all strangers. All had made a trip that distanced them from their earlier homes. They had left the known for the unfamiliar.

Ava Johnson, now eighty years old, left Norway in her twenties with her husband and two young children. She recalled the physical details of the journey. A sense of bewilderment pervaded her recollection of the trip. So much of it was mysterious; and how long it seemed!

We started out from the fjord on the ninth of August, 1927. We were sailing along smooth seas all afternoon until we came into a very bad storm on the North Sea. In the morning when we got up people were lying down all over the place. Someone took me into a drugstore and got me those never-seasick tablets, so I wasn't sick, just a little bit of vomiting. We came into the Atlantic, where it was beautiful to start the journey: a very nice boat and good food and a nice bed to sleep in. But when we came to Newfoundland we came into the worst storm again. There was a man there who had been sailing for many years who said he'd never seen a storm like that. It was six days until we landed at Halifax.

We couldn't speak a word of English. They took us up to a big house up there where they handed out these little books. My brother was standing holding his and someone came and took it out of his hand, so it must have been something interesting. A man who had been home to Norway to get his family told me he would help me go and buy some dinner. We got a good dinner in a restaurant, pork chops and blueberry pie; lots of blueberries in Norway, but we never made pie out of them.

They had boxes for all the immigrants for the train, a shoe box with food for two dollars, with jam in it and bread and other things. We had to sit on the hard wooden benches on the train for eight days, and there wasn't much to see, just stones and small houses, not nice ones. But when we got far inland in Canada, there they had nice gardens and there were lots of fruit trees in the valleys.

They took us to Montreal first; three days later we came to Winnipeg. We lay in the station there, waiting for a train to come and shovel us on like a

Cavalcade of loaded wagons near Wainwright, en route from Vermilion, Spring 1906.

bunch of sheep. We got on a train with soft benches, like sofas; I put my little girl down to sleep right away. The conductor came and told me we were in the wrong car. So we had to get off and get on the immigrant train with the hard benches.

We ate the bread we had for a day or two, and then we had to go eat in restaurants. That cost a lot of money. I felt really sorry because there were lots of people who couldn't afford to do that. One lady there was, with six children and ready to get another one. She sat there with all the children around her in the little compartment. She ate the jam and bread and had it all over her face.

Then, over this long Saskatchewan prairie, one house here and one house there. Three or four days we were sitting. When we came farther west it started to look more settled. We came to Hardisty at three o'clock in the morning. We had been sitting on the train for four nights and didn't have a sleep. We got to the farm about five in the morning.

Mary Morgan made the trip from England as a child. She recalled some of its disagreeable details:

❧ I sure remember that trip in 1909. We had no water half the time and my dad had to go to the diner and get my mother a cup of tea. My uncle made matters worse; he was just young. You see, we had a little coal oil stove, so we were going to do our own cooking on the train because you couldn't possibly afford to buy cooked food for six children. He packed the food things for us, and he packed the little oil stove in with our food. Well, I guess because of the shaking of the train the oil can ran over, so we ate bread soaked in coal oil for two or three days. It wasn't very nice, but you couldn't get anything else.

Violet McKnight recounted the story of the train trip to Edson, which was the railway terminus. Her family of five was heading for Beaverlodge, in the southern Peace River country, to farm. During a late and snowy evening, as we sat before the fire in her home, the family log house now expanded, she told me about the journey from Edson. Good humor— laughter and chuckles of appreciation for the family's good sense and dumb luck—pervaded her account, fraught with potential disaster though it was.

❧ We left Ontario in 1912, coming to Edson by train. There we bought a buckboard and a team of oxen and a grubstake. We left there in June because you had to wait until the grass grew. We had trouble at the Athabasca River.

We were moving up a hill behind a team of horses that belonged to a man from Hamilton. One of the horses kicked the ox and damaged his gall bladder. We waited two weeks in Athabasca. The ox died so we had to come on with the one ox. We met a family that were coming to take up land; they had one ox with toes broken from pulling loads up the hills. So they put their good ox and our live ox together and we came on with half a load. Mother and Father had to walk from Sturgeon Lake to hurry because the time limit for filing for the homestead was running out. We arrived here in the afternoon. Father got off the wagon and said, "If this metal peg has the number of the land on it, we're home." He said we could camp on the little lake on the back of the land, or we could stay on a little sunny open piece of prairie. We put up a tent.

The cows had been walking for so long that the next day they were ready to start again. The rooster was used to traveling too; he left our camp the next morning, and they had to go way out around the lake and finally bring the rooster back. It had taken us six weeks in all to get the three hundred miles to Beaverlodge.

For Edna Stanton, departure from England meant exposure to the peculiarities—to her, the vulgarities—of bizarre local custom. The trip went well until she left Edmonton by wagon.

On my way up north here I stopped at Mrs. White's shack. There were big cracks in the walls. And somebody else had the bath meant for me. There was another couple who said I could share theirs! I was horrified. Next morning there were twelve or fourteen men eating their breakfast. One man had a whole pile of pancakes stacked high, with bacon on top of that. He picked up the syrup jar and poured its whole contents over it. I was staring. Two RCMP policemen both started laughing. I suppose I had such a terrible look on my face. They asked, "Have you never seen anything like that before?"

When I asked for hot cakes—I didn't say biscuits—they brought me a plate of pancakes. I said, "I'm sorry, I didn't want pancakes, I wanted hot cakes." The cook said, "Well, this is what they are."

Then, nostalgically, she added, "My first Sunday, I was sure I could hear the church bells ringing. I had lived in Croydon, out of London. Every Sunday I'd feel a little annoyed because I could hear the church bells ringing; they were so real in my imagination. But they gradually died."

For some women the sound of the bells and all they represented did die

away in time. Other women, sometimes unwilling and sometimes unable to adapt, wistfully heard the resonances of earlier times all their lives. Grievances, injustices, anger, or misgivings color their recollections of the migration. Their reasons for arriving sometimes evaporated into a sense of futility when expectations never materialized. Yet more and more women came, for numerous reasons, which many of them recalled. Katherine Forman came as a child, her father drawn from the United States by the siren call of the west.

❦ My father was the one that turned the first sod here, practically. I think the idea of getting rich quick called him, though his health wasn't so good. He had a collapsed lung, and the doctors said that the different climate might help him. And of course there were a lot of others coming to the prairie at that time, so he wanted to try his luck, too, I guess. Mother didn't like the idea of him selling their home and leaving, but Dad had the urge like a lot of others. I know Mom sold her maple bedroom suite that she often mentioned would bring a fortune now, and I know the dining suite was sold and things like that, because they knew they'd have no room. You know how it was long ago: the man was the head of the house, especially as far as the Methodist religion was concerned. So it was a great sacrifice on the woman's part. It was the call of the west for the men.

Joanna Ricci's father came west also, to the mines at Canmore, not drawn so much as pushed out. Her phrase, "We couldn't make it down east," was often repeated by other women. The new environment, they hoped, might be more promising for coal miners of Italian origin.

❦ We came from Springhill, Nova Scotia, which was the very end of the world, in '22 or '23. My dad borrowed the money for a train ticket to come here, and then he paid it back. When he had enough, he sent for us. He had left us kids without a mother down there, all by ourselves. My mother had died, and we couldn't make it down east.

The Stedmans, a Jewish family, also left behind less than nothing, escaping from a population that graphically and violently expressed its hatred of them. The family arrived in Calgary, from Russia, in 1912.

❦ We had lived through pogroms. I can still feel the shaking arms of my mother around me, grabbing me, and hiding me. Many people came with a socialistic background from Russia. They wouldn't serve the Czar. To my eldest brother, to serve the Czar was a crime. He was to serve in the army, taken through the town by a police escort, but he escaped and they never caught him. The police escort was so incensed that they came into the house and took things away from us. We had a samovar that they took away. We had really nothing left in the little village.

Clearly, some migrants came simply because they had to. Ava Johnson delicately told me this poignant story about a pregnant girl she met on the long voyage over. She wondered whether the girl's life in the new country was better than the one left behind.

Coming from Norway to Lougheed in 1927, I picked up a girl on the way. She came in with us. She had problems and had left home, so I befriended her. At the train leaving Norway there was a boy talking with her who asked me if I could take her with me because she had to go; her dad said he would rather she were dead than have the baby. She was supposed to have some relatives in Canada. When we got here she stayed with us for a few days. Then some neighbors, maybe five miles away, asked if she could come and help there. She worked with them for a while. A man who used to sell fruits and clothing, traveling around, used to stop at that place. They arranged for her to marry this man. She couldn't speak a word of English, and they hadn't told her of this arrangement.

She had a wee baby boy. They were living in one room near Edmonton someplace. I guess they had hardly enough to eat. She once told me she wasn't sure if she should go to Canada or if she should jump into the river, but she decided to go. Just a young girl she was.

Women were sometimes drawn west by the urge for adventure, just as many men were. That desire in men is well documented, among women less so. Sarah Wilson, born in Ontario of an English family, was able to act on her impulse for excitement by finding herself a job, a teaching position in a small town. She doubts that her family would otherwise have let her go. When she married some years later, she gained a mother-in-law who shared her slightly mischievous adventurousness. I wish I had heard conversations between the two of them!

I came to Alberta in 1922. I had been teaching in the east and I saw an advertisement in the Toronto paper for a teacher in Lethbridge. I thought it would be a way of seeing the west. My ambitions at the time were to go all the way up to the Yukon and do a little traveling before returning, though I got sidetracked and never went back east.

My mother-in-law came when her husband, who was in the lumber business, had to leave Minnesota to go to Texas or Alberta. He had a choice. Dad said to Mother, "Now which do you want?" "Well," she said, "I'd rather be killed by Indians up in Alberta, Canada, than by rattlesnakes in Texas."

Another former teacher, Lily Dawes, had difficulty finding a school in the east. The prospects looked better in Alberta. Intimidated at first, and frightened by many new and strange experiences, she stayed on nonetheless, "and I'm here yet." Her fears, expressed in the following passage, both of the first black people she ever saw and of the roughness of the new country, came with her from her past, and in time dominated her less. She remained a teacher for many years. Other women like her who came alone, following their own impulses, offered the new society both their wit and their intelligence.

I couldn't find a school in Ontario in 1925. Mother and Father were dead; I did have two sisters. So I went over to Buffalo, New York. I was working in an office over there when I heard from the archbishop that teachers were scarce in Alberta. I arrived in Athabasca on the eighteenth of April.

It seemed like a wild country. Coming up on the train the lady in the seat ahead asked where I was going to teach. When I told her she said, "You're going to a colored settlement." Well, I had never seen a colored person in my life. The old folks used to tease you, scare you about colored folks. Well, "I'm going back," I said. I found out that the colored people may be black on the outside but they're white on the inside. They're very nice people. Still, it turned out I wasn't going to a colored settlement at all.

In Edmonton they told me it was another twenty miles; turned out it was over forty. The mailman was so overloaded I had this delivery man drive me. The roads were only them Indian trails then. I sat in the back seat of the democrat; it was raining and snowing that day so the delivery man gave me a raincoat to put on over mine. It took two hours to make the Athabasca hill.

We came to places where the bridges were washed out and the water came up to the bottom of the democrat. That wasn't all. The next day my future brother-in-law, though I didn't know it yet, came down to Athabasca just to get the mail, not expecting the teacher. He'd brought a team of young colts, breaking them in on the buggy. We went over half a mile of corduroy with this team of unbroken colts. You may know what that was like. I got into bed that night and cried! I thought, "I'll get one month's wages and I'm going back. I'm in no-man's land." But then I started to teach school on Monday, and I'm here yet. You get accustomed to it.

Ida Bronowski came because she had heard enough about husbands disappearing in the New World. Determinedly, she gathered together her belongings and her babies, and left Poland forever in 1922. Not for her, the pathetic figure of the abandoned wife!

I come to join my husband twenty years old. We married home. I not trust let man go away by himself. I say, "No, if you go, go together." I hear lots in Poland come from Canada, they talk. Man stay in rooms there, he forget wife and kids. I not trust.

Elizabeth Hanson, speaking in the soft, sweet voice that came with difficulty from her tiny body, at ninety-two lying blind in a hospital bed, was nonetheless just as indomitable. In Scotland she too had heard the stories about husbands who might leave and might forget. "Women have to look after themselves," she decided. And she did—looked after herself and her babies whom she adored, and her husband whom she also adored. Her little hand delicately stroked mine as she described the matching outfits, lovingly made for the babies, so that they would be proud on arriving at their last stop. Her hand stopped, as if breathless, as she recalled the station at Calgary, the mud and the wooden planks and the noise. Her small voice, almost the voice of a child, spoke.

Edinburgh was to me quite a wonderful place but there was a mania for emigrating to Canada in 1911. It seemed so rosy, and one made the other itch to get over here, and work was very, very scarce in Scotland. I loved my husband enough to rough anything to be with him. He wanted to come out ahead of me and find work and send for me. No, I wasn't having any of that. I'd heard of women being left and they never came back to get them; you were never sure. So many young men came over to Canada and some of them forgot to come back, not perhaps intentionally, but something happened that they couldn't come, maybe finances, or maybe finding another woman. I wasn't going to be left stranded in the old country with two babies and another on the way not knowing what my husband was going to do. Women have to look after themselves.

We sold our very nice home; we had a beautiful red leather sofa with oak frames. Before leaving I had special little outfits made for my children; they're very close together, fourteen months between them. They were darling, and I dressed them up on the train before we landed at Calgary station. The coats were beautifully made of the same material. I was so proud of my two little ones. But, oh dear, I saw what I had landed at! It was rather forbidding; it was dreadful. It was a wild country in those days here, not unruly, not unsafe, but nothing was completed. It was a raw, man's world, not for women. At times I was pretty broken-hearted, but it was my own doing. I could have stayed in the old country but I'd preferred to be with my husband and rough it with him.

So the women arrived, prepared to rough it with families or husbands or alone, sometimes horrified by what they found, sometimes delighted, often innocent, naive, and uncertain.

When we got off the train, coming straight to Calgary, we stood there; we didn't know what to do with ourselves. So we see a Mounted Police there, and my husband says, "Excuse me, could you tell me where I could get a room for the night for me and my wife? We've just come from England, and we're going to Uncle Johnny and we've got to let him know we're here." "Well," he said, "It's getting late now. How about if I can get you a room for the night and we'll see you get out tomorrow." The policeman went all over the place and couldn't get a place for us to go for the night. So he took us and gave us a beautiful supper and he said, "Would you be offended if I offer you a place in the jail? It's a good bed and there's nowhere else." We said yes, but I nearly died! Imagine, our first night we slept in jail! My husband offered him some money, but he said no. "You hang onto your money because you're going to need it."

Glimpses of utterly strange ways, foods, and landscapes awaited women on their arrival in Alberta. Ina Feiner recalled reaching her destination with her mother and her siblings. Her father had come earlier from Finland to work in the coal mines, and had now sent for the family.

I leave Finland the day that *Titanic*, that big ship, went down. Mummy's friends in Finland say, "Don't go those old ships, go the new one." Mother said, "I not go that new one; old ship is good enough for us."

When we coming here I was twelve years old. I never see train or engine. And you know what kind of feeling that was. The engine coming; I went to my grandma and I hold my grandma's arm and say, "Grandma, take me back your place. I can't go." I cry and cry. I prayed that train stop there. They said, "Come on, you like it." It's all right then. I never see orange or apple in Finland. This fellow give me orange. I went to Mummy and I said, "What is this?" She cut it and that's the first time I have orange. Also we buy tomato, but one bite and we throw it out the window. We buy bananas in the train. We didn't understand to peel them. When you bite the skin you don't like it. Mummy open that train window and I throw the banana away.

My dad, he worked in the mine. When we come they went and tell Dad. He always said, "My three girls coming and my wife." They run and tell Daddy, "Three girls not come, just come two girls." They turned one back in Liverpool because her eyes; she come a year later. I remember Finland so bad I not ever go visit. My husband can go if he want, but not me. I remember those ugly herrings in salty water; they get too old they get yellowish. I remember the yellow skin and yellow cheeks. We have good time here, because I have so good memories of my father. He bring whole box apples on his shoulder. He say, "The girls going to get all the apple juice they want."

A stopping place on the way to a new home, near Edson, 1913.

In 1923 we went up the northern Peace country, to Fairview, forty miles from the end of the steel. I remember the day I went in. I had traveled all night and half a day on the train. The baby got train sick. At the station my husband hired a fellow with an old Ford car with the tippy top. I was sick when I got there; the tipping top on the car bothered me. When I got into the house I went right into the kitchen. It wasn't hard to find; it was just a little four-room place. I looked up at the west window and there had been a big hole in it, mended with a metal piece, and all around it the glass was cracked. The patch was as big as the palm of my hand. I said, "Now, what a way to patch a window." My husband said, "That's where they shot at the last man." He explained to me how there'd been a lot of moonshining being done up there and this minister had taken some of the fellows to court about it, to Peace River town about sixty miles away. The bachelors decided just to scare him out. He was stirring cereal on the cookstove, a little iron four-lidded stove, and the shot came right through the window and grazed a door frame just above his head. There was the window as a reminder. Well, it really colored my views of the place. I thought, "My, what a place to come and bring a young child." Oh, I wasn't sorry I went. I enjoyed it finally, but that silly window upset me so.

When my husband's mother came out she had quite a time. She had been a cook in London and had some pretty nice places in good houses. Her husband came out in 1892 with the boys. She came out in '93; she had the other boy who would be about three years old and quite delicate, and a year-and-a-half-old girl. She said they lost the rudder when they were some miles out from Canada, and the ship cruised around for quite a while. They sent for help to a—these are her words—to a man o'war. They sent a pigeon out. Then she landed in Halifax. She had a sickly boy, a little girl, and the baggage. A man who had a horse and rig came up to her and said, "You give me your baggage checks and I'll look after your baggage for you." That was the last she saw of it. That was her introduction to the country.

They homesteaded out east of Innisfail. She said they couldn't even grow potatoes when she first came because they got frozen. There was nothing. She had to do something to get something for the kids to eat, so she went out and did washing and scrubbing in the Hudson's Bay store. She could get a sack of flour for that. She used to work for a couple of families too. The homestead was a sod shack with a straw roof and every time it rained, which it did quite often, there was a pool of water underneath the table. I guess she got fed up, and I guess her husband wasn't too good natured, so she went back to Calgary and she never lived with him again.

The railroad was right at the back of the house. She said that all the trainmen were good; they shoveled off a bunch of coal for her. She did washing for some of the men. They'd throw it off, and she'd do it and give it back. Some of the children went to school; the oldest one even got to high school. But my husband never went. He was working in the brewery when he was about eleven years old. He was a bit slow at learning; and then his mother had to work so hard. I often think what she must have gone through.

In 1913 we came to Edmonton from France. His decision, it was. He wants to be free; he's that way. He wants big spaces, he wants lots of room. Wilderness, he liked, and it was wild here. We stayed in Edmonton two years, but came north here. Even twenty miles was too close to people. But Grouard, where we went first, was too wild! He cussed the sixteen-mile portage from Smith Landing. He walked for thirteen days out of Edmonton, to Lac La Biche, looking for a homestead. "Lots of jackfish there," he said, "so you can come."

Group of Polish settlers, Sundance, 1929.

Everything was so different here, strange, even the food and the drink. We were used to wine and here they were giving us tea or coffee. The food wasn't cooked the same way. Dried fruit hadn't the same taste. The butcher for fresh pork was twenty-five miles away. So we had to do like the rest: the salt pork and the salted butter and the dried peas.

It's an irony: if we had stayed in France he would have been a front line soldier, ready to be killed. I was pregnant two months, and had a boy; if we were in France he would have been in the second war. That's why many people left the old country. They were so tired of all these wars. We were free here, but I was lonely. When I was too lonely I would go to the lake on our farm and watch the ducks and those little black things with white, the mud hens. Herons, too, and gulls; I would watch what they were doing and feel that I had company, and then I could come back home.

Mother said she cried for days because there was nothing green. The first year it was so dry; nothing. And when she saw a mustard plant with a little yellow blossom on it, she picked it and brought it in and put it on the table for flowers, because she always loved a table center.

My mother and my two sisters came to visit me after I was here about ten years. I came in 1914, and people didn't travel much. Mother didn't like it. Too barren, no trees, too much hard work. I can remember her telling me that I was so hard on my hands. She said, "You're going to be sorry. You're abusing your hands." And I did abuse my hands, washing on the board. She'd say, "Hang the clothes out even if they're not clean, rather than taking it out on your hands." But I'd want them white and I'd wash them. She said she wouldn't have done that, or liked it. And I didn't blame her. There was nothing to make her like it, nothing to make anyone like it.

My mother had lived all her life in Toronto. When my father came out here with the army in 1913, we never intended to live here; we were always going back to Toronto to live. My mother was a home person; her home was her life. Out here we lived in lovely furnished homes. She didn't have to change her mode of life, except it wasn't her own home. We had our furniture in storage for ten years in Toronto. We were always going to go back to Toronto to live.

We left Russia in a period of deep famine. We were starving. The only thing that saved us were parcels of food. Members of our family were already swallowed from the hunger. I was pretty pale when I came, and undernourished. I was sixteen and I looked twelve. Naturally, coming from the conditions we experienced, it made me so assimilated and happy just to see the beautiful food that was served here. And then the clean house; I came to my sister's and had a bed to myself to sleep in. Here I had pajamas and a nice bed. My sister was very kind to me.

❧ If you come to a new country, everybody's got to take their chances, and you've got to make the best of it. You can't be too different, and you can't be too exacting about the differences. You have to go along with the others, otherwise you'll have too much division. Of course I kept to my own; maybe I still do.

I brought my china with me. That black and white cup there, it's hundreds of years old. And the teapot was my mother's grandmother's. The little pink one just up there was my grandmother's when she was a little girl. The tankards are the King and Queen, King Edward, at their coronation. My father had them given to him and then he gave them to me. This cup, the blue and red one, one Indian used to come around and when he saw it he insisted on drinking out of that cup. I told him I didn't use that cup. He couldn't understand anybody having cups around and not using them. That was his cup.

❧ My mother made up her mind that she was going with Father and the family and that was it. Her friends in Ireland tried to dissuade her. They said, "Sarah, don't you think it extremely indiscreet and unwise to take all those children and go out to a country like Canada?" I know she missed her friends, but she never grumbled.

The winter of '06 was one of the worst in the west. It was forty below for six weeks. Mother later said, when asked how she lived through it, "Oh well, I thought this was Canada!" One great roan steer, that first winter, with great horns came close to the house and waved his head; he put his head through the window. It was at night, so Mother had to take one of the pillows off the bed and stuff it into the window.

I can still remember Mother's trunk and the wonderful things that were in it. Her old wedding dress was one of the things. It smelled of mothballs. The trunk also contained very soft, colorful embroidery silks. Sometimes on the dull days when we didn't know what to do, we'd ask for the silks out of the trunks, just to feel and look at. Mother would pick them up gently with her sore, cracked fingers.

❧ I was four years old when we came. Mother didn't want to come; she didn't want to leave her mother and her sisters. She had a good boarding school education. She had left a beautiful, beautiful home in Ontario. There was nothing in Calgary like it. I remember her crying her heart out all the way out on the train. It seemed that it took so long to come. She brought a piano out here. She would sit down at the piano every night, play "Home, Sweet Home," and cry. She was so homesick. I can still feel her pain.

I didn't have too many people to leave behind in England, just a brother who was sickly from the fighting in 1914 and one sister who was a jealous kind of sister. At first, I thought we were never going to get by here, but we did. We made it, and we never regretted it. We used to sit and watch people who didn't want to work and be just disgusted. They didn't want to try hard enough. Me and my husband, we couldn't do that. We had to make a go of it, because when we left they all said, "You'll never make a go of it." And I says, "Well, don't you worry. We will never ask for anything."

Scottish women emigrating to their future employment as domestic servants, 1930.

The whole village in Oregon came down to see us off, my mother and us three girls, and thought we would be scalped the moment we arrived. We came to Empress. The cowpunchers used to come in and roar down the street. My mother was a good Presbyterian and said, "This is no place to raise daughters," so when the steel came through to Calgary she was the first one on board. She went to the Land Titles office, put her finger on the map, and said, "I'll take that." It was forty-five miles from town in the dry belt, eighteen miles from a river, ninety-five miles from coal. Mother insisted that they build a house for us on this land. It was a shack really, so small we didn't think we could get into it, let alone the piano. There were three things my mother would never be detached from: her piano, her library, and her sewing machine.

After 1929, the migrations to Alberta slowed. By then the land came to seem less a frontier, the society not so transitory. The women came during the settlement years, eager or reconciled, to make a home. Some came without possessions and without ties, to form the environment into shapes that would be comfortable for themselves. Others recreated the scenes they had known before with pianos and libraries and sewing machines. By will or by chance, with forethought or by accident, they came to work, to raise children, to sew, cook, farm, clean, and embroider, and to form new communities.

The immigrants on the frontier would shape the land they came to as surely as the geography and climate influenced it. They would also create a culture. Some would try to reproduce familiar social structures, while others would try to eradicate the known in hopes of a better life. They would participate in political groups and economic schemes. They would work the land, earn money, and lose fortunes. They might participate in a city's growth or live in utter isolation, spending years alone on a homestead. The long trip over and done, here they were on a frontier, prepared to create a new society, a culture they would form and which would, in turn, form them.

GIRLHOOD

any of the women I interviewed came to Alberta as children. They provided me with descriptions of frontier childhood, both urban and rural—rich glimpses of their first twelve years. While their accounts were sometimes idealized, their early life misted over by an urge to reconstruct perfect families, even nostalgic reminiscences were revealing. What seemed to them the best kind of family and childhood was in any case a reflection of their own childhoods. Other accounts revealed anger, sometimes bitterness. Candor informed all the women's narratives, so that we can begin to get a picture of frontier girls' childhoods.

Childhood was the period of life most overladen with tradition, when parents hoped to form their children into the kind of adults they wanted them to be. Most often their vision of that adult was not based on the world as it might be twenty years later, but on a nostalgic memory of the world as it had been during their own childhoods. They assumed, perhaps even expected, a future not unlike their own pasts. Adults tended, then, to raise their daughters in conservative ways. And yet, these were people who had themselves broken radically from the past to come to a frontier. They had arrived not only to establish something new, but often to leave behind something old, something that didn't work for them, something too rigid and confining. They were often seeking freedom, and yet they expected a traditional relationship of obedience and authority with their children. Frontier parents tried to teach girls to behave in ways that reached back into their own, their parents', and their grandparents' childhoods. Girls of all ethnic backgrounds and social classes were supposed to learn obedience to their parents.

However, the unconventional environment also exerted itself. The open land, for one thing, with its possibilities for running wildly and freely, and seemingly eternally, offered girls a glimpse of something like freedom. The uncertainties of crops, of weather, of schools open one term and closed the next, and of money, created the knowledge that life was transitory and fragile, not well grounded in past certainties. Obedience to hierarchy was a bit harder to instill in frontier children than in children growing up in more settled places. Even as girls were studying their future roles, they also heard the whisper of the inappropriate.

Girls felt conflicting desires both to accommodate and not to accommodate their parents' expectations. The first usually prevailed. Most of them described their families as supportive and strengthening, though by no means free of conflict, and recalled being, for the most part, obedient. Families at their best represented order in a shifting, uncertain, and often scary world. The link between parents and children offered daughters a sense of stability and of continuity with a past that might otherwise never be known. And yet, the potential for disorder beckoned. Mischievousness, rebellion, resistance, and sometimes outright hatred were voiced by women recalling their frontier childhoods. Let us listen to them as they reminisce.

Looming large in many women's minds as they thought and spoke of their childhoods before 1929 were the chores, which were the most essential representation of order. The children's labor was essential to the economic welfare of most households, especially rural ones. Vivian Russo, when remembering herself at ten, sixty years earlier, told of gathering fuel on the woodless prairie. Her experiences were echoed by many other prairie women who worked as children.

Down near that Montana border it was very flat. It was a long way to get any coal, sort of barren; no wood around, so we used to hire a stoneboat and go out and pick buffalo chips. People say now, "What in the world is that?" and I tell them, "Cow dirt." You went out and when they were dry you picked them up, and if they weren't dry you turned them over and went back. It makes wonderful fires, and it's clean. When it was dry there was no smell. My uncle had a lean-to with a sliding door into the kitchen, and we stored them all in there. You pulled out two or three, set them up in the stove, lit a match to them, and they started just like nothing. A really hot fire, good for baking.

Farming in the dry prairie south, wheat and cattle farming mostly, demanded the participation of children where paid labor was unattainable. Wilma Post was born in eastern Canada and came west early in her life. She described her early participation in the family farm as quite routine, and her world as secure.

When I was twelve years old I was out stooking grain. My dad threw the bundles into the rack, and my sister and I would take turns at cutting them with a sickle blade, which is a sharp blade cut on both sides. We'd cut the twine and then feed it into the threshing machine by hand. Then Dad would go for another load, and we could have a little rest till he'd come back. That first threshing machine was fed by hand. The next one that I remember was the old steam machine, and boy, you didn't have to cut bundles for that; you could feed them in. So this was progress, and in those days we were looking forward to something that was going to make life a little easier.

Still, I believe we had a carefree life until the '14 war came along. Even during the war years I think I was too young for the real impact of it. I know there was a workload to carry. But it was removed from us. We used to have to make wash cloths for the war and to help knit socks at home. Mother would teach us to go a round or two on a sock.

And then, as though irrelevantly, though the link was clear, she added, "Today, children don't know which direction they're going. Our world wasn't so expanded." Indeed.

Bronya Lubitsch expressed her resistance to chores, shared by her siblings, though she felt sympathy for her mother along with considerable anger over the family's travails.

Sometimes when you'd put a cow to pasture it'd get loose, and then you'd have to go and pay a fine. Every night we'd have to get the cows from the pasture with the fence. There was so much trouble over those cows. Daddy would say to the boys, "Did you go and get the cows?" They would always say, "Well, I went last night; now it's his turn." In the end Daddy went mostly, rather than listen to the boys argue whose turn it was to go.

Once Dad got a load of hay for the cows. Ten dollars, a lot of money then. Mama was expecting one of the babies; she was sewing, making diapers. My brother got a wooden match; I don't know what made him go to the barn and set the hay on fire. It all smoldered. The cows wouldn't eat it any more after that. Mama was just sick over it. She had to go to the hospital early.

Girl feeding cattle, Jumping Pound, during the flu epidemic, 1918.

I remember her sewing always. The cleaning was my chore, and the others would deliver milk. Everybody bought milk and cheese from my mother, so it would be a quarter here and a dime there. Then we had the chickens, close to a hundred, and a turkey. Once my brother was taking care of a friend's husky dog. He tied it up to the fence. We all went to bed. In the morning there were a hundred dead chickens, and that one darn turkey the only one standing.

Elizabeth Woychyk was so dextrous in her sewing that she was released early from other household chores so her needlework could bring extra money into the home of a coal miner. Despite her skill, she did not enter the needle trades, but stayed close to home. Her talent did not become a job later in life. She took great pride in her skill and still continues to do exquisite needlework.

My mother wouldn't say so, but I knew that when I was sewing I was doing something good. Let's put it this way: that dressmaking came very easy for me. I went to the machine when I was ten years old. My youngest brother had a long, crisp christening dress which I made into a short dress quickly. My mother was sometimes afraid that I'd get a needle right through my finger, but she let me go. When I was twelve I could sew a dress. I got some pink plaid and made a dress with a sailor collar. I didn't know how to embroider but I put on pink smocking: why I'm telling you this is because I'm surprised at myself. I think I'd have been a dressmaker if I had had a chance.

Childhoods were also filled with the kinds of incidents—accidents, holidays, narrow escapes—that become the memories of old age, the kinds of stories one repeats to one's children and grandchildren. Viola Carter's tumbled out, one after another, in the firm youthful voice that belied her many physical infirmities. She was born in Denver, Colorado, and orphaned at six months. Her grandmother, a widowed Catholic then fifty-three years old, left her home in Pennsylvania, fetched the infant, and moved to northern Alberta in 1900. Life was too hard for the two to sustain themselves in the small town, so they left for the city.

By the time I was eight I was living in Edmonton. I used to go visit my aunt and uncle in the country in the summer—never in winter because the winters were dreadful. All the kids slept upstairs in a huge room. They had those old iron beds, about five of them, up there. There were no springs, no mattresses; they would buy ticking and the kids' job was to fill them with straw.

I remember the straw coming through the ticking, kind of scratchy. They eventually had thirteen children, and they've all done well. There were just five of us then.

Their nearest neighbor was a Russian fellow. My uncle had planted his crops, which were usually very, very poor. This year it was a little better than usual. We children went out in the wheat field one day; Uncle Jim was so proud of it and so happy that it was coming along so nicely. What did we little devils do? We laid down one after the other and rolled through. We rolled, one after another. We kept going and going. We ruined about six acres, just flattened them, broke the wheat off right to the ground. It was almost due to be cut. He never knew that we did it, and we were too frightened to tell him. We heard Aunt and Uncle talking, and the more we heard, the more frightened we became. This is where the Russian fellow comes in. He had a team of oxen and a stoneboat. He'd walk behind them and throw the stones on the stoneboat. Well, my Uncle Jim said that his team of oxen got loose and ran through the field and that he was going to sue him. Of course, poor old Ivan swore up and down that the oxen were never loose. However, Uncle Jim could never believe anything else. I think it was thirty years later that I told him. I've never known anyone to laugh so hard.

My Uncle Jim was the kindest, dearest man, and with all that family I never knew him to get angry. When he was in trouble, or sad or things were going wrong, he'd always sing. When I hear country music today, it's my Uncle Jim singing. Only once did I ever see him mad. We were told never to go on the haystacks, which were built up so that if it rained or snowed the rain or snow wouldn't get through the stack. We dug a hole through the middle of one, and then crosswise, and then down from the top. He was really angry because we'd ruined his haystack. The hay was so precious to them.

One Christmas I was there, with Grandma. There was a railing on the staircase going up to the great big bedroom where we kids slept. Christmas Eve, we all hung our stockings on this railing. My poor aunt didn't know where we'd hung them and thought we'd forgotten about them, so she piled everything on the dining table. All the toys and candy and everything they could afford were there. You can imagine the blank faces of all these kids coming down the stairs, their empty stockings hanging there. We all sat down so glum. First we cried, then we started to talk. We decided that we'd all been bad kids and probably Santa hadn't come, so we'd have to be better next year. Well, when we went into the kitchen, there it all was, of course, laid out. My aunt felt terrible about that. I didn't get very much that year because Grandma hadn't taken anything down with her, and of course my aunt had so many kids of her own she couldn't afford to buy me anything. Back in Edmonton my other aunt had bought me this little doll about eight or ten inches high with a beautiful red dress with gold braid on it. It was tied up at the top of my bed. I never forgot that doll; I was ecstatic over her.

Before moving to Edmonton, Grandma had about a dozen or so hens. She used to save the eggs up, and I'd take them down to the store and trade them for something she wanted. Old Mr. Turner was awful mean, a great big fellow.

Group of Sarcee girls, Sarcee Reserve, 1890s.

Maybe he wasn't so big, but I was small and he looked awful. Once I brought home a piece of meat that was spoiled. Grandma told me to take it back. He shoved ten cents at me and said, "Tell your grandma I don't want her nickel trade." He was the only store in town. Grandma had to go down and plead with him to forgive her. He was a mean old thing. He sold heavy farm machinery; had it out in the backyard behind the store, and had a barbed wire fence all around the place. Thought it was secure. One Halloween during daylight, one of the boys unfastened the fence. That night about twenty of us, quiet as could be, pulled all the machinery out and took it down the middle of the street; just left it!

Grandma also had some turkeys, the old gobbler and five or six turkey hens. Every time I'd see the old gobbler chasing the hens I'd go in and beat him off with a stick. Grandma used to put out settings of eggs and all the eggs would go rotten. She could never figure this out. I don't think she ever found out why she didn't have any fertilized.

One day I left the gate open after I went in after the old gobbler. He was kind of a mean old fellow; I went after him with a stick, and he came after me. Furiously, he chased me out of the yard, and I can still remember running down the main street yelling, "Old Gobbler! Old Gobbler!" He followed me for two blocks. I finally ducked into Turner's store. That's the way I saved my skin!

Grandma was so old, so I had a lot of chores to do. My uncle used to bring in sleigh loads of poles, poplar trees, I guess, about eight inches around. He'd leave them outside our house. I had an old Swedish saw, and I'd put the green wood up on the sawhorse and saw it. One day I picked up the axe in the cold wintertime and put my tongue on it to lick the frost off. I went crying into the house, the axe against my mouth. I couldn't get it off. Grandma poured cold water on it and it came off, took all the skin with it.

We had one cow, an old farm cow, old Blossom. She didn't have any horns. Oh, she was the love of my life. She'd graze in the fields, and I never had to go after her. I'd just call, "Blossy, Blossy." She'd come to meet me, and I'd ride her home. She wouldn't let anybody else ride her. When we were moving away, Grandma made me drive the old cow up to the stockyard. How could she? That was the saddest thing in my life, I think. It wasn't fair to ask a child to do that. I loved that cow just like a sister or a brother. I had no one else, you know, just Blossom. I was blind with tears all the way up and back. Blind with tears.

To carry with us all the yearnings a child's heart desires: we all try to call to mind our childhoods. Incidents from a city childhood in 1915 were warmly remembered by Doris Spring, who, of a middle-class Calgary family, described herself as a "playgirl."

We used to bobsled down the street for blocks. The firemen would cut off the cross street. You'd lie on the sled, twelve of us, and go like the devil. The only street that wasn't cut off was Seventeenth Avenue, and we just had to hold our breath as we went across, hoping that nothing was coming. Traffic was mostly streetcars, and by that time we were slowed down enough that we could roll off if we saw something coming.

Barbara West's mischievousness emerged over and over during her youth. All her life she remained as spunky, outspoken, and unbowed as she was at the age of eight.

I remember a very funny time when Grandfather and I had started off to walk down to the Cathedral in Calgary. He used to walk down there on Sunday morning, all dressed up just so, the white spats and the cane, and always the morning coat; all dolled up. We walked down past the Holy Cross Hospital, all mud around it and just a little wooden sidewalk. I was flipping along; I jumped on one end of the board, it flew up, and he went sprawling in the mud!

She told me another incident from her childhood; this one didn't amuse, but horrified her.

Our family doctor was a fiend from hell. My father was a great friend of his. I don't think my dad ever realized what was wrong with the guy. I'll tell you: he was a dope fiend. It was because he'd been on a hospital ship in the Dardanelles during the war, and I know that man worked night and day. He broke himself down. I hated him. He would ask my father if I could go with him while he tried to collect his bills; he wanted people to think he was married and that his family was starving so they would pay him. One day my mother sent me with a cake or a pie or some damn thing, down to his office, and this is when it happened. He tried to rape me. I was ten, probably. I was absolutely frightened. I didn't think my parents would believe me because they had such high respect for him; they'd think I was making it up. Nowadays a girl wouldn't feel like that, would she? She would tell. I think they're more aware of things like that.

Dorothy Collins treasured the memories of her childhood perhaps more than most people because they lived on as a contrast to her present. Born in Ontario of an old, established family, and "much petted," as she said, she moved to a northern hamlet of perhaps one hundred people as a young bride in 1918. Her husband farmed there, but not very successfully, and while she doted on him and her children, she never felt comfortable among her farming neighbors. They, in turn, thought she put on airs. She was waiting for me on the front steps of her log house the morning I went to visit her. She wore a pretty navy blue dress and black rubber boots, for

Daughter of an Anglican missionary on a swing, with her Blood nursemaid, Waterton Lakes Park, 1920

she had just been out in the woods picking white wood violets for the table. As I approached on foot, she pointed at the acre or so of prairie grass before her home, the house set against a blue-green backdrop of pine and birch still shining from a recent rain shower, and said, "You know, I had a wonderful husband and wonderful children, but I never had one thing that I always wanted—a proper lawn." The only tangible reminders of the civilization she still yearned for were the beautifully carved oak sideboard and the silver teapot she had brought with her, and the grace of the white wood violets.

I was the youngest in the family, and thoroughly spoiled and petted. I lapped it up. Mother took me to her home when she found out that her mother was very ill. I had a white rabbit fur coat, and the mailman said he was going to put me in the mail bag, and I believed him. Oh, I was scared!

Childhood could also include much frustration and isolation. Margaret Jones escaped these in her daydreams and in her fascination with plants and animals. Her early interest became the motivation for studying science at the University of Alberta. She was one of the first female students there.

The intrusion of English people in Calgary, a Scottish city, was resented deeply. I felt this as a child. Sometimes it was painful. They used to throw stones at me, at school. Most of my schooling in England had been of a high standard; here they put me into grade two, though I could do grade six work, and I used to be shooed up to grade six every now and then. That didn't make me any more popular with my school fellows. There was a beautiful stream behind the school. In the stream were little plants growing with tiny—oh, you could call them moons that caused the plants to float. Oh, was I ever in love with those! The kids came and I tried to show them how beautiful the floating plants were, but they just threw stones at me.

One boy used to like to put my hair in the ink, but I didn't mind that at all. My hair was down below my waist, and that hair was just plain cruelty. Finally my mother had it cut off when I was seventeen. That was a very joyful day as far as I was concerned. Still, I had been romantic about my hair. I had imagined that, sooner or later, I would be allowed to join the army, and then I would ride boldly on a horse with my hair floating behind me. You see, we'd got women's suffrage, and there was no reason to believe that we wouldn't be going into the armies.

Fantasies about horses and armies, strength and freedom were essential escapes for many girls on whom obedience was impressed. Only small resistances to discipline were possible for most of them.

Family rules were being on time for meals. That was very important. Mother would call on the phone—we had a phone early on—wherever we were and say, "You must come right home." It was always Mother you went in to, because often Dad was late too. And bedtime: very regular bedtime. My mother played the piano quite well and at night, to put off going to bed, we would ask her to play "The Robin's Return," our favorite piece.

I can remember some good spankings. We girls always felt that our brother got away with murder. He did, too, because he was the youngest and a boy, and they had always counted on having a boy before they did. I started going to parties when I was about seventeen. A lot of the school kids went to dancing lessons before, but I wasn't allowed to, and felt kind of badly about it. And reading: I remember one time reading a book of Ralph Connor's and my father saying, "Don't read that rubbish," and taking it away from me. He thought it was too old for me. Ralph Connor, if you please!

I guess it was my mother who was involved in the regular everyday things, more than my dad. My dad laid down rules, about things like going to parties and reading, though Mother had to carry them out, if you know what I mean.

I was not allowed out at night, even in high school. I was not allowed to go to a dance without my mother. She liked to dance, too; my dad didn't, so she went. Grade eleven, grade twelve, it was maybe a little freer. But still, I remember having to be in at ten o'clock, and if I was a minute late that was just too bad.

I can only remember being slapped hard once, and that was for playing cards on Sunday. Mother loved to play cards, but on Sundays it was absolutely forbidden. Sunday was the dullest day. You couldn't do anything. But you know, if you did something objectionable to your parents they'd be dismayed that you didn't live up to their expectations, and that was just about as big a punishment as you could have. You knew the limits, and if you went beyond them their displeasure was great.

I can't say that my social life changed at university. I think we were still tremendously influenced by parents. We had a code that had been instilled in us; we were all still going on exactly as we would have at home.

The "code" that girls learned seemed to be taught to them mostly by their mothers. Many women felt that while their fathers imposed the rules, their mothers carried them out. Those rules were often different for girls than for boys, an injustice noted by several women. Barbara West of Calgary resisted and struggled all along.

A lot of my upbringing was left to my mother because my father was away from home a tremendous amount. This is where my brother felt that our discipline fell down. He said he didn't know what discipline was until he got into the army. But then, my father never questioned the boys or asked them to do any bit of housework whatever. I resented this greatly. We had a cabin up in Banff that my grandfather had built. All our friends from here would come to visit us, and there'd be stacks of dishes. I would be told to go and help the hired girl; the boys would never. Or I'd have to set the table. "Why can't the boys set the table?" Or the boys would be allowed to go somewhere that I wasn't allowed to go. I wasn't allowed to have a bicycle, and I was so mad. I had an awful time even getting a horse. It was all right for the boys, but when I started riding theirs then I got one. I guess I was expected to sit and play the piano, or embroider, or knit, or some damn thing. I resisted all along. I should have been a boy.

Certain places were out of bounds to me. I was not supposed to go to the Plaza Dance Hall because I was only sixteen, though when I wanted to go I did. My parents knew the man that ran it, and I was always scared he'd see me and kick me out. When I was sixteen I tried to pretend I was eighteen, like now I pretend I'm a few years younger!

I had one particular friend; I loved her and wanted to go to her house. But my grandparents were death on liquor, and I wasn't allowed to go. My grandparents felt they weren't our kind of people because they owned a brewery.

When I got out of high school, the first thing I wanted to be was a nurse. So I went to the family doctor, along with his daughter, and he told us, "Go home, the both of you." He was the same as my father, you see. "You'll be patients before long. You're not cut out to be nurses." So I went to business college and worked for a few months. My father didn't even know I was working; my mother was frightened to tell him because he would raise such a row. Then I got a job on the Chautauqua, and he phoned them up and said I was too young and got me fired. He told me, "You have to go in those awful hotels with bed bugs. There's not even a lock on the doors." "Okay. I'll stick a knife in the door." But no ... Then I got a job peeling potatoes in the YMCA hut up at Banff. He wouldn't let me do that either. He wouldn't let me do any of those things. You were just supposed to sit around the house until you got married. He wasn't even going to let me drive the car. The boys could drive, but I wasn't allowed. Finally, I took the car out one day and just went!

🌿 My father was very set in his ways. He was the head of the house. I think a lot of Dad, but just the same, as I grew older I realized it was not the same feeling as it was with Mother. She was more understanding and considerate. I could always go to Mom and talk to her, whereas with Dad I was always a little afraid. I used to say he expected perfection in everything. He was brought up in the way that what he said was law. He probably didn't feel any better than we did, actually. Even when I was older he was strict with me, didn't want me to go to public dances and things like that. There were times when I had rather a guilty feeling, but I used to think, "I don't feel I'm doing any harm." As I grew older I became a little more independent.

Women rarely spoke as warmly of their fathers as did Myrtle Smith. Her father was a missionary teacher who moved his family to a Blackfoot reserve in 1905.

🌿 I know in our family my father was very good with us kids. He waited on us and looked after us, and if we were sick, well, boy, it was always him that wanted to hold us and doctor us.

More often I heard stories that indicated a distance between fathers and their children. Few of them were as filled with rage as Joanna Ricci's.

🌿 My father didn't want me going with no boys; he had a glorified idea that the minute I got out the door alone, I was going to come home and bring him a baby or something. My intentions were nothing like that. I came home one night and he waited for me in the dark, and he bashed my face until the blood was all over the place. He saw somebody walking along a railroad track and in his drunken stupor had thought it was me. This is what I had to put up with. But you live through it and you survive. You get tough.

I had to go and ask for permission to get married because I wasn't old enough, and he says, "Okay, I'll sign the paper. Just get out of my road. I haven't got you to worry about now."

Conflict, hatred, fear or guilt, or a mixture of these blended with love or pity—Millie Melnyk was motivated by all of these feelings during her difficult early years. And to them she added despair.

Sarcee child, Sarcee Reserve.

In the beginning, when they first came to Hardieville, my mother said there was hardly any homes at all. The grass was so big—I was probably three years old—and I got lost once in the grass so that she had to look for me, it was so tall. Later on the grass would be right into the yard. We had to go a mile or two to the river, up on top of the coulee and down to the river. My father loved fishing. He used to make nets for others. The men would go with the nets and get fish. My dad was great with us children then. He would take us during the summer holidays down to the river. We'd take cans from lard— ten pounds, five pounds, three pounds, and so forth—and he knew where the saskatoons grew, and the gooseberries, and the chokecherries. Then if there was a creek, or just a little puddle of water that ran out from the Old Man River, we'd go in and wade.

Two girls examining the remains of a farm implement, probably early 1900s.

I was a tomboy. I used to like to play marbles. They were made of clay. The ones made of glass we used to call shooters. There'd be a different saying for the different ways you were shooting. There was one saying, "Nuts on you." My father heard me saying that. I had a little velvet bag I'd made, with about eighty marbles and a few shooters. My father took that bag and he threw it away. I cried a lot. Later on we were cleaning out the stables, which had a lot of wood that my mother had carried from the boxcars, and I found that little bag.

My mother used to send me with my father when he picked up his paycheck because often she couldn't leave the children and the boarders. At first he would take five dollars and say, "Don't tell your mother," and he'd give me a quarter. Ten cents was an awful lot of money, and a quarter was really big. He would say, "Don't tell her because you know Mother would get mad, and you don't want that," so of course I wouldn't tell. I would just come home. Later on it was ten dollars. Then he would go into town and gamble. They'd let you win so much, but by the time you got home you didn't have anything. My uncle and auntie did know because my uncle would take the same pay as my father since they both worked in the mine loading coal. One time, I remember I told him, "Father, you are taking too much," because I knew arithmetic well. I did have a lot of fun being a child, though when you think of it I wasn't so much a child. I was more mature in a lot of ways.

One night, my father lost the money and he came home. My mother had only ten dollars left after we paid the bills. It was about eleven o'clock at night and we were all sleeping. My sister slept with me in one bed, and the two boys slept in another. The youngest slept between my mom and dad, and that wasn't a big bed, just a three-quarter. They were arguing; that woke me up. My mother said they had lost all the money he took home; in fact he earned quite a bit more than my mother ever knew. In fact, up until she died she didn't know how much. I would never have told her. So I remember she started crying and she threw the last ten dollars on the floor. He took it and went. I was crying, I'll tell you; I must have been eleven years old. You grew up with this and you saw. The other kids were asleep, but I was the one who saw.

While the relationship between daughters and their fathers was supported by the mythology of the frontier family—fathers were the undeniable heads of households whether they worked or not, whether they were kind or cruel—the bonds between mothers and daughters were closer and more emotional and intense. Even if mothers did not wield public authority, they were able to assert their presence in an immediate way in

the home, the realm within which they could play out their own needs for action. They often had more impact on their children's lives than fathers had, despite men's presumed power as the head of the family. Some daughters like Millie Melnyk grew up to examine their relations with their mothers closely and often unsentimentally. From her introspection she derived strength, pain, and finally compassion.

My mother didn't know how to read or write, but believe me, she had a way with words, and right to the very end. It's hard for me to tell it in just a few words because life—well, she had a story of her own. I know at Coalhurst, when it would often be hard and the neighbors would come, the other women, and she sat for a little while gossiping, she would take about an ounce of whiskey and that would just make her go at times!

My mother was sure strict, because she had made a mistake. She liked the boys better than the girls. At that time she didn't say much, just mentioned once or twice that she would talk to me. When she had the last baby I said, "Gosh, why so many babies?" And she says, "Wait until you get married and you'll see." I say, "Oh, no." She says, "Well, what are you going to have?" I said, "I'm going to have four and that's it. That's all I'm going to have." I didn't know a thing, anything about it. This is what I was. She laughed at me often. Often she would say, "Rather a stone born than a girl." And you know, when I got married I wanted a girl, deep down, more than anything else. I know what she went through, that she made a mistake and was so afraid to let me go, or my sister. I often wondered, and then later on I understood why.

I'll tell you an instance. You know, everyone swore at their children, and they called them the first thing that came in their minds, a word that in Ukrainian meant "whore." My mother didn't say that much. But there was this wedding once, and she got mad at me for some reason. She says, "Whore" to me; I was fifteen, sixteen. But I said, "Well, Mother," in Ukrainian, "how do you expect people not to call me that when my own mother's calling me? If anybody heard this that's what they would think, too." And she started to cry, and she says, "Look, I didn't mean it. It's just a word, but I don't mean it." Since then she never called me that. But it's just one of those things, and I never held it against her, even then, to be honest, never. I'm glad that I understood from what it came.

Intense admiration, loyalty, devotion, and respect permeated other lovingly recalled accounts. Theodora Wade praised her mother first by quoting a neighbor who had recently told her, "You know, you had the most wonderful mother I have ever known. How she did it, I'll never know." Mrs. Wade agreed; she certainly had cause to. Her mother and father had arrived in Edmonton in 1905, he to work for the railroad. One week after they had stepped off the train with their six children, he died, leaving her in a strange city with no resources. She resolved not to return to the east, found a large house to rent, and took in boarders to meet some of the family's expenses. The older children found work. She then began serving hot meals at noon to men working on construction in the area, adding income by taking in laundry and sewing for other people. Her daughter perceived her stamina and determination. "It was hard on her, being left like that. But my mother was very proud. She would work herself to the bone, but she wouldn't go and beg for anything, no sir." A lifetime of admiration and love emerged from the relationship between mothers and daughters. Those relationships were the basis of a strength they would often call upon.

Schooling was another aspect of childhood that many women talked about. Most of them had gone to schools in their areas; few girls were sent away, since most families did not insist on more education for their daughters than the district could provide. Sons were more often boarded at school. Many settlers' accounts include a glimpse of a son leaving home for the first time to go to school, yet rarely do we hear how the boys themselves felt about it. Albertan women spoke of the experience of leaving home for a distant school. For Margaret Furness it was a formidable experience, plunging her into a world that intimidated her at first. She described her journey to school as a girl of fourteen.

My first five years, spent on the prairie, were nothing very exciting. I was sort of a timid child, I realize. I was even afraid of the chickens. It seems so ridiculous now, but I was afraid of everything. It was a very lonely feeling. I spent a lot of time reading, and we spent hours crocheting and knitting and embroidering. Even our underwear and nighties had to have fancy lace on them.

I was sort of overprotected too, I guess. The first time I went away from home was to go to the Alberta Ladies College, which was operated by the Presbyterian church. I had to wait for a night train, and the head of the college was going to be waiting for me in Edmonton. The train stalled somewhere, and they couldn't get heat through to the cars, so we had to double up with some of the others in the sleeping compartments until they got another engine out from Calgary. We got off at Munson, finally. If you've ever been to Munson you know the long steps you had to go down from the station to the town. I had to stay overnight in a hotel. I'd never been in a hotel, but I guess the Lord was with me. Still, I was just terrified.

There was only a traveler and myself, and maybe another man. My parents, of course, had warned me not to talk to strangers. It was dark and, of course, the town wasn't lit up. I felt that, well, I've just got to fight it out, so I started toward the hotel. I went in the door of the hotel; of course I was a stranger. A crew building the grain elevator was staying there, and of course they were all making remarks about this young lady. But I never let on I heard this. The man at the desk told me there was a room I could have upstairs. I went up to my room; I was so nervous and frightened. Something told me to move the dresser up against the door. I hadn't been in bed any time at all and I heard somebody rattling at the door. I was shaking like a leaf, and hungry, too. Suddenly I saw eyes looking in at me through the glass over the door. These men said they were going to have a dance downstairs and wanted me to come. I never answered; I never let on I heard. I just lay there petrified.

When I got up in the morning I was afraid to go out the door of the hotel. But all this time I had a protector. I didn't know it, but it was the commercial traveler, who said, "Don't you be afraid, lady. I'm watching over you. You're perfectly all right." I got back on the train, and the head of the college met me. Was I ever thankful, because I didn't know what I was going to do! So, it seemed it all worked out.

Beatrice Wentworth attended the same school some years later. At twenty-two, she was delighted to be getting some education.

🍂 My mother wasn't well, so I had to stay home from school from the time I was twelve. Then I determined I was going to get some education, so my sister next to me stayed home and helped. I went to the Alberta Ladies College, built for girls like myself from small places where there was no high school. Did I ever enjoy my two years there! At first I felt lonely; they put me in a room with a twelve-year-old girl, and I was twenty-two then. I didn't intend to stay, but as the days went by I just loved it. It was the two most enjoyable years of my life. We had wonderful teachers. The second year I took two violin lessons a week, and I took both French and Latin. I got grade nine and ten and that was as far as I went, because the rest of the family needed an education.

If they went to school at all early in the twentieth century, Indian and Métis children almost invariably attended mission schools. Belle Harcourt, a Métis woman eighty-five years old when we talked, recalled her schooling in the Slave Lake area as an experience not unlike imprisonment. Many other Native women echoed her sentiment, based in part on the separation from all that was familiar and comfortable and on the cruelty and trivialization they experienced in the schools.

Hungarian children, 1920s.

Young woman, seventeen years old, poses on her saddle horse, Strathmore, 1908.

Everybody's kids were in the mission school because there was no buses, nothing to travel with to take the kids to school. They had to be in there. People wouldn't see their kids at home all winter; they came from way down the river where there was no school, just trappers. You go in September, come out next June. My mother, she was about four years old, about the first one there, and stayed about fourteen years. Some kids never go home. Summer holidays they're there; they don't have anywhere to go. But she had only two grades or three. The first years you go in, you do A grade: that's hardly anything you learn. The next year is B, then C, then grade 1. They're just teaching you English, I guess.

You weren't allowed to talk Cree in front of the nuns; they don't understand. Outside you could, but not in front of the nuns. The sisters were pretty strict; that's why I never cared for them at all. If somebody done something wrong and doesn't come out and say, "I did it," we all have to stand around, not move for hours. We don't play; we don't do anything.

The sisters take care of the kids. Something wrong, they tell the father, the priest, and that was really something. You were scared of the fathers more than the nuns. The priest comes in and gives us hell or straps some kids. If it's a boy, he was brought to the girls' side; he has to kneel down over a chair and the father straps him. And if it's a girl, she's taken to the boys' side, and all those boys standing there and watching her get strapped. It makes all the other kids get scared. Some would run away; they run home.

Millie Melnyk had mixed feelings about her schooling, which ended in grade eight. She lived in an ethnically diverse coal-mining region. Schools in such areas played an important role in homogenizing the outlook and manners of the population, in teaching them "Canadian" ways, though the students often paid a high price in alienation. The women's recollections of schools frequently concerned their struggle, often futile, against limitations, their tensions between the urge to fit into the new environment and the need to maintain familiar ways and some independence.

I didn't know a word of English when I went to school at five. I remember the first day, I started to cry, and Mr. Cameron put me in the chair in front of his desk, the chair he used to sit on. He gave me a book to read, and I remember looking at the pictures but the tears were coming down. The Italians, or Hungarians or whatever, they didn't know English either, but they taught us first to sing. We sang in the morning and before noon. I learned all the Scotch songs and all the Irish songs. And of course you had to sing "God Save the King," all for learning English.

In grade four and five I had a very good teacher—cranky, we called her an old maid, but very good. She used to take us out on the prairie and down the coulee and show us the different flowers. One time I got the strap from her. Sometimes it would come up to your wrist, or if you pulled your hand away, just on the fingers. I had a second cousin next to me. She was a lot older, and things didn't come easy for her. At arithmetic I was very good, so she asked me for an answer. The teacher heard and said, "Stay after school," and she gave me two straps on each hand. Another time—I must have been twelve—in the hallway, one of the kids took off his toque and threw it on the ceiling and it made a mark, because the ceiling was all dirty from the dust of the coal furnace. It made a mark, and gosh, it was fun. So I threw mine. When we came in the teacher said, "Who threw their toques up there? Stand up." So we all had to stand up. That's how I got the strap twice.

Later, when we moved to Hardieville, we used to catch the train to school. The miners would go on Number Six, then they'd fill the cabooses with coal. We would get on with the coal and jump off the train here, where it would slow down. I had a wonderful teacher then. She would read from *Little Women*

McDougall High School Commercial class, Edmonton, 1916.

a little bit each day until we finished the book. The teachers used to come out and play baseball with us, and in the wintertime we'd make snowballs.

The English history was easy because it was about the kings and queens, how they lived, Henry VIII and all that. But the Canadian history was very dry; there was nothing in there. The only thing that was hard for me was grammar. I could draw the North American map and put in all the rivers. But grade eight they didn't have, so they had night school for about two months and that was it. They had no more. That's how come I had no more school.

Joanna Ricci also felt alienated from her classmates and teachers in a predominantly Mormon school. She ascribed her difficulties to the rebelliousness that she maintained even as an adult, but her experiences were not entirely unusual. They were, in fact, shared by other women unwilling to fit into a pattern not of their own making, a pattern designed to make them like everyone else. They resisted.

I quit at grade nine. I had trouble with one of the teachers, this young fellow just out of university, and he didn't know any more about teaching than I did. And too, Magrath is a Mormon town, and if you weren't a Mormon you were an outcast in the whole school. You were second-rate citizens as far as they were concerned. One teacher, when she wanted to punish a boy, would make the boy sit with me. I never took part in any activities except with my girlfriends at home. I only had two real girlfriends. One was a Mormon, but her father drank so she wasn't popular, and the other girl had had trouble, too, so she wasn't popular, and that's the ones I associated with. It sure made you feel very small and rebellious. Let's say I was a very rebellious character.

For many other women the desire to attend school was intense and urgent, and sometimes achieved at great personal cost.

I have a cousin who's eighty-four now. She was always very clever and read a lot. She had to go to Edmonton and work for her board when she went to high school. She had no picnic, I'm telling you. The lady she had to work for really took a pound of flesh. She had to get up in the morning and pare the vegetables and get everything ready for the noon dinner. On Saturdays she had to clean the place from the top to the bottom before she could eat lunch, and then she was to go shopping for the woman. I never could have done it. She must have been a strong girl or she never could have stood it.

The public school was often the institution through which the immigrant children first learned to become part of the new land. Girls absorbed language and cultural habits, shedding some of the patterns and anxieties of their pasts.

🌿 I went to maybe grade eight in Russia. The children were rough, and especially to the Jewish children. We would be scared to walk through the streets. I started here in grade seven, just sitting and listening because I couldn't speak a word. I lived with my sister then, who clothed me and provided for me. The people around me at home spoke broken English; from them I learned Yiddish. At school the students were very nice to me, but I felt self-conscious because in grade seven I was seventeen. Toward the end of the year I was passed to grade eight. I graduated high school with high marks.

Reading provided girls with another route to growing up, to learning to become adult, to expanding their vision. "Every Christmas we used to get the *Girls Own Annual*. It gave us a glimpse of life that we weren't used to here, the sophisticated English life." As a mode of education and socialization, reading was less filled with conflict than was going to school, since it was a solitary activity. Girls could plunge wholeheartedly into a book, enjoying it as pure pleasure and learning from it. Parents disapproved of some authors or subjects, but on the whole books were encouraged.

🌿 We had to be in bed quite early, and I'd read and read, and at last I'd read so long I'd just fall asleep. The book was on my chest, and the light still burning in the lamp. Dad would come home from the night shift and Mother would say, "I bet Lillian's going to be a minister because she's always got a book!"

🌿 When Mother came from Ireland she brought dishes, curtains, a great mahogany wardrobe, and every book she thought would be useful. I read the boys' magazines and books like *Boys Annual* and *Chums*. I remember reading *Pilgrim's Progress* in an old hard binding when I was twelve. We used to read to each other at home on Saturdays while Mother sewed. I think that any child who is never read to suffers real poverty.

Books fed the curiosity and the imagination. "When I was cooking in the hospital I used to read all the doctor's books whether I was supposed to or not. About appendixes, how they took them out, things like that, and I used to get scared to death in case I was going to get all those things." Books could also point toward political goals. "When we came here," said Katja Cohen, "there was a group of progressive Jews who formed a literary club. We tried to bring speakers and had lectures and concerts. It was a sort of socialist group." Finally, books began to move the young girl towards landscapes far larger than the horizon she could see with her own eyes.

❦ We had a very good reference library at home, including the *Encyclopedia Britannica*, published in the 1890s. It was very useful. If somebody said, "When did Milton live?—of course everybody knows that—we'd go to it. There was a very good collection of novels and poetry. That was our salvation. We got our political ideas from other people and from books. We didn't have radio, but we got journals and we read the books. People from the trade union movement in the States and from Britain came over, and some of them settled here in southern Alberta. Tolstoy's books had a very, very wide influence on hundreds of idealistic young people. I don't think so much of him now, myself. He meant awfully well, but he couldn't work with other people. That, to my way of thinking, is the only hope for the world, for people to work with each other.

Frontier girls absorbed roles, skills, duties, and responsibilities from their parents and their schools. People tried to teach them what they should become as adults. Obedience and docility, though, did not come easily to many of them. Lessons taught them were not necessarily received or acquired, either in part or in whole. Frontier children were not passive listeners or helpless recipients who would in time become what others intended them to be. Instead, they brought to the process of growing up their own resistance and rebellion, intellect and imagination.

The frontier environment exerted its influence. Openness, potential, and rapid growth all contributed to the possibility for a future very different from the present. Girls certainly absorbed some of what they were supposed to learn, but they just as certainly resisted and even rejected some of it—not all girls and not all of the time, but often enough that the rest of their lives might not conform to old ideas of appropriate female behavior. New possibilities were glimpsed by girls growing up in an untraditional environment. Some girls in time ignored most of the chances to explore, while others understood and acted on their subversive possibilities. They began to get glimpses of new ways of being women.

WOMEN and MEN

Once childhood was over, there was still much for a girl to learn. Young women had to further refine their knowledge of the behavior and sense of self appropriate to their femaleness. Part of that knowledge, gained during their adolescent years, was their sexuality. They needed to find out about what most of them called "the facts of life": menstruation, conception, and pregnancy. The next stage lay in experiencing these biological realities as they matured in their twenties, for most of them married and had children, often more children than they wanted. In growing toward adulthood, they would need to learn too about men, how to adapt themselves to men's needs, how to suppress their own, and sometimes how to acknowledge their own desires.

The women with whom I spoke were quite frank and open about the first stage of their adolescent lives, even if embarrassed at times and delicate in their language, using euphemisms or simply leaving words unspoken. Their occasional reticence revealed a lot about their socialization as women: they had learned to conceal their bodies, even to be ashamed of them. Where variety informed other aspects of their lives, where experiences were so varied, a curious similarity pervaded women's recollections of how they had first learned that they had female bodies. "Learning" perhaps implies more consciousness than is accurate, for rather than knowledge, it is adolescent ignorance and female shame that emerge from their accounts.

My first menstruation came on the day of the Sunday School picnic, and I was very much put out. I can remember my mother saying that every woman has the same thing; she explained why, real quickly, and that was it. I was told just that I was growing up and there would be a change.

Relatives and peers hinted now and again, indicated that "something would happen," and that this mystery of blood had something to do with becoming a woman.

The Métis mothers used to tell us to expect it; it's a sign of blood and that's a sign you're a girl. But I wouldn't tell my mother. I thought it was dirty. Everybody goes through that. I went to the bathroom and saw this blood, and started washing my clothes and hid them before my parents came home. I was scared something happened. That same year—I was thirteen—I was in the convent and the same thing happened. I woke up and my sheet was full of spots. No pad they gave you, just bloomers. You had to wash your things. The sister let you sleep that morning. I thought I was doing something wrong. You feel guilty.

In Russia I knew nothing about this. I was hiding it and I was scared, scared to let anybody know this was happening to me.

The hints about menstruation were usually imprecise; the menstrual taboo was powerful in frontier society. The menarche, the beginning of menstruation, was a moment denied, relegated to a realm where fear and shame ruled. Women learned at an early age to hide signs of their female-ness, their bodies, and their selves, agreeing obediently to play parts in scripts they had not written.

My aunt told me about menstruating when I was about nine years old. She was sixteen. For four years I worried about it. She had explained that some day this would come and not to be frightened. So every day of my life, for those four years, I'd look to see if everything was all right.

I was thirteen and in the classroom. We were dismissed and I got up; I had on a white summer dress. The girl behind me pulled me back into my seat and whispered to me, "Don't get up. I'll get my coat for you." "Why?" "You've got something red on your dress." The teacher dismissed the class and I sat there. She said, "Rosalind, why aren't you leaving?" "I can't." "You'd better go." I put my head down on the desk and started to cry. The teacher came down and pulled me by the arm, trying to pull me out of the desk. I just hung on to the desk. She couldn't figure out what in the world was wrong. By this time Bonnie came back. She had to go home to get her coat. That's why it took so long. The teacher suddenly realized and left me alone. That was grim, what I had to learn as I grew up.

Many of the women, suffused with shame at what they saw to be nasty but also inevitable, were prepared by that shame to suppress voices inside themselves that called for self-love and pride. Not all of them, of course, were prevented from joy or productivity or creativity. Margaret Jones, with her usual good humor and quick intelligence, channeled her curiosity into a world that for her grew larger and larger.

❧ Mother was very shy about acquainting one with the facts of life. She did say, "Someday, there'll be blood on your nightgown; let me know." And I thought that had to do with something mysterious. That day one of my friends told me that babies are carried around in the mother's abdomen. I told my mother that, and she at least told me the word womb, but that was about all the instruction I had. I find that passing on gossip at school was the commonest method of instruction.

I started out to read Darwin with the purpose of finding out what was what. The more I found out about controversies surrounding books, the more likely I was to read them. Of course Darwin and the rest of them assumed that people knew everything about the facts of life, so they didn't mention that. However, the most vivid religious experience I ever had was when I finished Darwin's *Descent of Man*. I can't think of anything that influenced me more deeply than that. I got out of bed and thanked God for evolution. It confirmed everything that was beautiful.

Things came together in a nutty sort of way. The first year I was teaching I had a nice, quiet old gelding to ride. He was a darling, even when he bounced me off. I was no athlete as you can imagine! He would come back and sniff at me and you could almost hear him saying, "It's come loose again." The next year they didn't want this heavy horse out of service so I got a little mare. Her name was Lady. She galloped much more and didn't bother to see why I'd come loose. I didn't know the horse was in heat. A stallion came into the yard after her and I realized almost immediately what he wanted. The stallion chased my poor Lady and caught her. I can still see those hooves up above my

Stony Plain couple, c. 1913.

head. I got two or three of the bigger boys to help me, and we managed to get Lady away from the stallion. I trembled: what would the owners say when I got home? As a matter of fact, they were delighted to have an extra free colt.

My big aim was to keep the kids in my classes from knowing what was happening, for I still thought about my mother's statements about it being naughty to know too much. I've had many experiences that have made me realize how wrong I was.

Most women learned that it was just as well not to know too much, and especially not to talk about sexuality. They learned to become ashamed and to think of themselves as unlovable. Most of them, if they learned it at all, discovered their own desires late in their lives, often only after sexuality no longer seemed to threaten.

Sexuality was indeed threatening, not much to be welcomed in a world in which sensuality played a small role. Pleasure in scents, in touches, might be acknowledged when aroused by baking bread or by the yellow crocuses emerging through wind-crusted snow, but rarely did frontier women express sexual pleasure, inappropriate in their frontier culture, which demanded reticence. An adult woman's life, entered into with some repulsion and much ignorance, would be an uneasy life for a long time.

How did I actually find out about sexual activity between men and women? It must have been from a neighbor child. She must have said something because I can remember when I was twelve years old we had a small house, and Father sometimes came home quite late because of his job. I woke up and I heard some kind of sound. I can remember the chills that went up and down me, the chills of recognition, really chills of horror. As far as sexual information was concerned, I think I was deprived, but not much more than the other people my age. We just had to stumble along. The worst of it was that I just loved to have a man's arms around me. That was everything to me as I got older. Being hugged and kissed was just the most marvelous thing that could happen to me. But I couldn't ever admit this to my friends. I think it would have been much better if we had all said, "Isn't that just it?" But we didn't. This marvelous part of growing up would have been so much easier. Instead, I thought there was something wrong with me.

Prohibitions against contact with men were freely passed along, though rarely explained. Either fathers or mothers might convey the rules.

Whether Scandinavian, Ukrainian, or Anglo-Canadian, ethnic background seemed not to alter the lessons that parents wanted to impress on their daughters.

🔥 Sex was not a discussed topic. My father once said, "Thelma, I don't want you to do anything with anybody else that you wouldn't do right here in the living room." I didn't know what he was talking about, so I just said, "No, of course not, Dad."

🔥 Mother used to tell me after I was a little bit older, "You're going around with the boys; don't ever give in because then you'll be pregnant. Don't let them touch you." So I can tell you, when a boy touched me, I sprang back. I remember one fellow said to me, "What's the matter? You got a spring?"

🔥 We were so naive it was pitiful. My grandmother taught me the Ten Commandments. When we came to "Thou shalt not commit adultery," I asked, "Grandma, what's adultery?" She slapped me! Then she said, "Never ask that question again." All she ever told me later was, "Keep the young men at arm's length." That was her way of telling me to protect myself.

Barbara West told me, "Sex certainly wasn't one of the major things on our minds." No, indeed not. But their lack of knowledge might have at least one predictable outcome, as she indicated in an incident drawn from her convent schooling in Calgary.

🔥 No, all I can remember is Mother Theresa at the convent telling us not to speak to people on the street. Reverend Mother had raised a little girl whose mother had died and whose father put her in the convent as a boarder. Reverend Mother adored her. She went to Normal School, and by Jove, the first thing that happened was she got pregnant. I don't suppose Reverend Mother ever told her anything.

The questions about birth were answered by a variety of fairy tales the settlers brought with them: the usual cabbage patch, doctor's bag, and haystack babies whose first cries resounding through the house caused children to scurry about looking for the new kittens.

🔥 I was so dumb I thought the doctor brought babies. One afternoon Mom was outdoors. She was feeling bad so she was out in the chicken yard walking around, because I guess she was going to have the baby. Well, my cousin said,

"You know what's the matter with your mother?" "What?" "She's going to have a baby." "You're crazy," I said.

Then my aunt came over. We were upstairs and we could hear a baby crying. All of a sudden Dad comes upstairs, and he says, "Girls, are you awake?" "Yes," I said. "There's a baby, isn't there?" "Yes, you better come and see your little sister." Well, all the rest of us were blond. But she had dark hair and dark eyes, lying beside my mother in bed, and we were looking at her, a sister. My cousin was kind of slow spoken. We went upstairs and she said, "You know, your dad said that's a sister, but she sure looks like a nigger baby."

Girls moved toward adult life—more precisely, toward marriage, by which they would be defined as grown women. The tentative glances at boys or men, slowly reaching out to communicate with them, were a major, if mysterious, part of their adolescence.

I know when my husband was courting me he had just a little buggy and a horse. I'd be so scared of that horse. I met him the first time at the third house from our place. It was just a shack with two rooms. They were moving it, and I was watching, and he was watching me. I didn't know that at the time. Later on I met him at a dance and he says, "You're the girl that was watching," and I said, "Yes, they took our playhouse away." It was empty so long that we used to go out there and play house and hide-and-go-seek. I felt so sorry for that house when they moved it. But another house sprang up there.

Well, 1905 was a hard winter, '05 or '06. There was a Montana outfit settled on the creek, just three miles from us. I think there were five or six men. They didn't buy much land, just a half section. They had a little house and were running cattle. They called themselves the Canadian Cattle Company. The second year out their foreman got killed. The team ran away while he had the tugs extended. The neck yoke on the wagon was too long and he was killed, going to Strathmore. So they asked my future husband to come to this cattle company for foreman, and that's where I met him, when he came over here to live. I was just at home at the time. There was nowhere to work anyway.

Boys began by filling only a small compartment of a young girl's life. Later, their presence loomed larger, as Barbara West of Calgary recalled.

I had my first beau when I was sixteen. He was a nice Catholic boy. I went with him for years, but I didn't marry him. He used to take me to the old

Pantages every Saturday; that was the vaudeville, and then he'd come home and have dinner. He got his money's worth, really. And then Sunday nights: Sunday was church night for everybody and I don't think it was for religion. It was to meet your boyfriend and then you'd walk home with him. We'd sit around the dining room table playing some foolish game, but Mother and Father were in the next room. I fell out with him later.

Girls became increasingly aware that their future lives depended on their interaction with men. They could barely envision a life on their own—and quite sensibly, since so few doors were open to single women. They began to go out with men and invite them home, most often with the expectation of marriage. Certainly, parents expected that this would be the end result. Very few of the women remained single; most of their parents had encouraged them to marry in almost the same breath as they warned against intimacy with boys. In the countryside or in the city, young women needed men, if only to ensure some kind of economic future, apart from a desire for intimacy. Yet those very people who would be so essential in their lives were also so mysterious, so different from themselves. One's behavior had to alter in their presence, sometimes in very puzzling ways. Arleen MacKnight, who grew up in an isolated hamlet in the north and later went to Athabasca to work, found herself treated in a way that made her feel unlike herself. She found when going out with men that she was expected

Swiss immigrants on their wedding day, Hillcrest, 1929

to act different from her accustomed mode. Relating with men meant relating with people who had grown up with different expectations and life experiences. But they were the ones who could set the terms of the relationship; most women could only agree to them.

My mother married the oldest brother. He had a younger brother, Tom; Mother said I'd be safe with him. He would be about twenty, I guess, and I would be sixteen. I was never treated so royally in my life. It seemed that he took a very great liking to me and I wasn't used to this. It was like a prince conducting a queen. I thought, "Boy, I guess I'm some kid." He went off to the army then, and I left town to work in a real estate office.

There was a man in the office who was a—what do you call a man who examines rocks?—a geologist. He used to phone a girl called Madeleine. There was something about her; the girls that I was living with were altogether different. I guess perhaps she was older, more sophisticated. She told him on the phone, "Tell the girl that's in your office to come over this evening, too." The gentleman asked me if he could take me over to Madeleine's. I was a little nervous because these people were older. I didn't know that when you are introduced to a young man, you just don't jump up and shake hands with him. This geologist, Leonard, said, "You're not supposed to do that. When you're introduced to a man, you only say, 'How do you do?' If you jump up and shake hands with him that shows that you're terribly interested in him." I said I somehow felt like shaking hands with the man. "Oh," he said, "you really have to be trained in etiquette. I'll have to teach you." And I thought, "You don't need to bother ..."

He took me out to dinner and in fact he proposed marriage. Of course he was going to have to train me to live up to his position, and he was about fifteen years older than me, and he'd been in the war. He said, "I would like to buy you a ring and we could be engaged." I answered that I was engaged to someone who was in the army now. Though Tom and I hadn't any formal engagement, the fact remained that I wasn't going to take up with anybody else until I saw what happened to him or saw how he felt.

Maybe I did need some teaching. I probably did. But I've never jumped up and shaken hands with a man since that day. Still, I don't know what harm there is in it.

Courtship eventually led to marriage, a union that sometimes followed more quickly than the couple expected, as Evelyn Appleby recalled.

❧ I guess back then girls and boys were sneaking around together at all ages, the same as they do today, you know, and there were goings on just the same as they do today. It wasn't accepted the same; it went under cover but it was certainly being done. They were the flappers, you know, and they'd be all dressed up and get most of the dances; they had a wonderful time and we were quite envious of them. Their parents weren't bothered too much about them, I don't think.

Certainly, there were girls pregnant before they married. But they were usually with the person they had been courting with. They would go out with a boy and get married. There was a certain amount of embarrassment if a person had to get married. Some people marked on the calendar when they got married so they'd know. It wasn't the accepted thing it is today, of course. There might have been some common-law people, sure, but young people weren't shacking up; it was down at the bush or someplace else. But I don't think there was so much of it because you knew everybody. I even knew the dogs' names, so you couldn't get away with very much.

Other courtships lasted longer, and some marriages were very carefully planned, as the following excerpts indicate. The first was recalled by May Potter, a Mormon from Utah who came to a Mormon community near Lethbridge with her college degree in teaching. Her marriage lasted for over sixty-five years of friendship and companionship.

❧ I began teaching in 1912. I taught for four years. One of the students in my class was a young man, but older than I was. In fact, I had a winter course in which I taught men who were old enough to be my father because in the wintertime there was not much for a man to do, and a good many of them had lost out on their educational opportunities, so they came back and took this winter course. He showed such wonderful capacity that I was just thrilled to have him in the class. I could see that there was a man who had the potential of being an outstanding man. It was his logical presentation of anything, a logical sequence of thinking. I realized that he had a naturally trained mind. He got interested in me, and I was naturally interested in him. So when he proposed I said, "Now, I do not want to marry you until you have your degree." All my life I never wanted to be in a position of the woman up here and the man down there. The man should have the ability to inspire confidence in his wife, and she should be able to appreciate him. Now, if she's had no education and he's had no education, Lord save them.

Couple from Viking, photographed in Edmonton, 1900.

When girls were educated beyond high school, either at university or at normal school, their marriages tended to be postponed. They delayed them because the women enjoyed their work, or because their fiancés, usually similarly educated, felt they could not yet afford to marry.

Very seldom did my classmates at university marry right away. The boys had to get established in their professions and everyone was poor as church mice, you know, so the girls taught or something until the boy was ready. Then they gave up their jobs and proceeded to propagate the species!

Class, family, and education often helped to determine who could marry whom. Marriages were sometimes a family's or society's expressions of suitability.

I know when we were kids we used to wonder about the teachers, if they ever went out with a man, or if they ever had boyfriends. The teachers around here didn't marry until pretty late, some in the fifties. I suppose probably being a teacher, and the men being mostly miners, perhaps they wouldn't dare ask the school teachers.

After the war, when the men came back, a lot of people were getting married. I met my husband when I was working in a hospital in Edmonton, where I continued to work for a couple of years after the war, so I did have a long engagement. In those days, men went to the fathers for permission. It was so different from now. There was none of this carelessness that there is today.

Millie Melnyk insisted on marriage on her own terms: "I won't marry unless it's the one I love." Resisting an arranged marriage was more difficult for her than for May Potter, who was well educated, or Constance Palmer, whose lengthy engagement was permitted by the habits of her class. Millie Melnyk had to struggle alone against parents and a society that insisted on marriage—any marriage.

I had an awful lot of boyfriends, young and old. The young ones were like brothers. There was one young fellow that I really kind of liked, and probably would have got to love, but my father didn't care for him. My mother used to be worried; I was seventeen, going on eighteen. She was worried I was going to be an old maid. She says, "You're too choosy; you're picking." I says, "If I live to forty I won't marry unless it's the one I love." I wanted somebody that I could really love. There was one fellow from Hillcrest who used to come, and friends of my father said to me, "I have a lovely boy for you," and all that. I was working then; I came home from work and we sat on the bed in the bedroom and talked a bit. And the first thing, he's asking me to marry him. I said, "I don't know you." He had lovely teeth, but he was kind of bald. He was a very nice person. "How about writing?" So his friend began writing for him. I remember he sent me a big box of chocolates, five pounds, for Christmas. I was really furious. I didn't want to take anything from a person. I gave it to my brothers. By then I knew what I didn't want. But I didn't know how to get off the hook because my father and my mother liked him. There were others before that I had refused and I had a hard time getting them to go. Oh gosh, did I have trouble!

Well, later I went to this concert. We had good plays, too, and an orchestra. And there was a young fellow; he was kind of shy and standing in a doorway. I wasn't interested in anybody else. How was I going to meet him? I stepped up to him and I said, "The concert was beautiful." This is where I began, because he had played the mandolin. So when he want back to his mining town, what did I do? I though of it in my mind when I went to bed and I think I gave it a week or two, a good week anyway. And I thought, "It wouldn't hurt me to write and tell him how nice the concert was, and if he cared to write back I would write again."

So I wrote this letter. Of course I tore up quite a few pages, but I finally wrote it so it didn't sound like I was trying to get him. It was just a perfectly friendly letter, just, "Dear friend" and "lovely concert." And I got a letter inside of a week. He wrote and asked if a person wanted to farm, how would I ...? He didn't put it right there, but I read between the lines very well. I wrote back and said, "If a person loves the man she's getting married to, she'll go any-where."

He could read English, and I could read Ukrainian. After that, I bought a mandolin for myself and I started going to school to learn more Ukrainian. About three months later he came back. I met him at the station. I walked with him right through the prairies. Well, I promised I would marry him and then I thought, "Gee, what if my mom and dad don't like him?" So I had plans to get some clothes and elope. I didn't even tell this woman I was doing housework for because I thought, "Who knows if he comes for me or not?" I was proud, I guess. It happens my father knew all about him; he and my uncles found out all about him, that he was a driver at the mines. We had a civil wedding.

Wedding day, the couple seated in the snow, 1900.

Henrietta Crow, a Cree woman whose family left the far north early in the century for a hamlet near Slave Lake, had no choice whatsoever. Her marriage was arranged by her parents in 1915, as her own mother's had been a generation before.

❧ Your parents choose the guy you going to marry. You don't even know the man. Here comes your husband; I was fifteen. The first dance I went to, when I was fifteen, with old Mrs. Williamson; her daughters were just young girls. Sara was my best friend so their mother came and asked my mother if I could come to the dance. But my mother had to talk to my dad first. Finally, after a week, my dad agrees so I can go with the old lady and her daughters. We walked all the way there, about six miles, to go dancing. The first dance I ever went to was at Grouard, maybe 1915.

After that dance, Sunday after, some people came to visit my mother and they were having dinner. I was in the kitchen washing dishes and all at once I heard my mother say, "Oh yes, she'll marry him." And that's it. And I'm wondering who was going to marry who. And it was me they were talking about. If you go tell your daughter now today, I don't know what she'd tell you. I didn't know anything about it. I was only fifteen. I still thought I was a kid, staying at home, never been with any guys, never been anywhere, know nothing, milking cows, get a pail of water, wash floor. And sewing all the time; your mother tells you, you do this and that. And all of a sudden you're getting married a year from now.

And all this time I thought it's not going to happen; they're just talking. About three months later I saw this guy come in; that's the man I'm going to marry. He sat there talking to my dad. I didn't even look at him, really. I didn't care to see him. I went to the kitchen. He's talking to my mom and dad. I didn't like him. Not like today; girls look at guys. We never used to care.

At that dance, I danced with him once. He talked to me; I don't know if I talked to him. Then I had to go sit down beside the old lady. So that was all. She'd let her daughters go with guys, take them home, but me, no, because my mother wasn't there and my dad said, "Nobody can walk you home." I said, "I don't want nobody to walk me home." I was scared of men, because I had never talked to any. That's the only time I talked to him; he came over about three months' time and sat there talking to my mom and dad, but I didn't talk to him. I went to the kitchen and stayed there all by myself. He's across the floor and I'm across here. Mostly it happened like that those days. My mother was married like that.

A very few women did not marry at all; some of them relished their freedom. Others, like Lizzie Helm, felt that in not marrying they were sacrificing something, "at least that's what a lot have told me." At another level, it seemed throughout her conversation that her self-esteem derived largely from that sacrifice, from looking after her brothers and her father, and from not having to confront the strangeness of men, of whom she confessed herself frightened.

I watched Mother so much. Learning about the house came to me from watching her. I used to cook, sometimes bake the bread. I can remember putting those little loaves in—we called it a Dutch loaf in those days—and I'd push in one of those minty candies and that was Father's. We had my father twenty years after Mother passed away. You see, I promised him the day she passed away to look after him. I did; I couldn't be married even if I was missing something. What would my brothers have done? They've been good to me. Richard said the last time he was up here, he said, "If it hadn't been for you, Dad would never have stayed." They might all have gone back to England or to British Columbia. So I've really in one way sacrificed; that's what a lot have told me. But I'm not sorry because the boys have been good to me. To be truthful, I think I was scared by men, kind of shy.

By contrast, Jehanne Casgrain was absolutely delighted by her marriages—all three of them! Now eighty-four, with sparkling, intelligent eyes and soft pink cheeks, slight and small, she has a husband twenty-five years younger than herself. She was the daughter of a couple who migrated from Quebec to Wisconsin and then to Alberta, there to establish a town still homogeneous today, French and Catholic. Today she is as lively and talkative as she must have been at her first wedding, seventy-five years ago.

It was a little log church right over there where I was married in 1911. You see, I was just fourteen on the day I was married; not a baby, I was mature. The years were quite full for me. Of course, now I'm older. My health is not so good. I can't do what I used to, but like I say, now I married a younger man than I am. While I was young I married an older man, and now I married a younger one!

Few marriages were undertaken in such a zestful spirit. More often, the women expressed something like resignation, as Inez Wood did.

🌿 We used to come for the weekend to my mother's and sleep there. That's how my first son was born in the same house where I was born. He was a seven-month baby. Everybody had seven-month babies. I don't remember if I wanted to get married, but love is a many splendored thing, eh?

Many accounts of getting engaged and married were oddly free of intensity, of either positive or negative emotions. One might almost add marriage to death and taxes as an inevitable, but not necessarily a joyous event.

🌿 My husband was out here in western Canada a long time. He went over to England in the war and he used to write me when he was away, because I knew him when he was a boy in St. John's. He'd tell me how he was. I didn't have any idea that I was going to marry him. He came home from war, and he still used to write me from the west and tell me the news. When he asked me to marry him, that was in a letter too, and he sent me the money to come out. Mother didn't like it very well, me going out so far by myself.

Wedding ceremonies and receptions usually conformed to ethnic tradition. Ceremonial occasions tended to be the instances in women's lives that were least changed by the frontier. Rural and urban people attempted to reproduce in ceremonies, through foods and customs, what they had left behind. Tradition provided the occasion with a sense of public validation. Marriages, births, and deaths were treated as events that were sanctioned by the community, and attended by neighbors and relatives. As nearly as possible, weddings resembled those of the old country, wherever that might be.

🌿 My wedding lasted for three days. I was twenty. An old-fashioned wedding. Imagine anybody having a hundred guests in a small house. My mother and her friends cooked for quite a few days, and no fridges then. She would run up and down from that cellar. They used to make really beautiful food.

🌿 Bob's mother put on a little wedding for us; with Bob having the grocery store, he was well known in the district. See, my parents were both dead. This probably accounts for the idea that I wasn't too lonesome when I come out here. As far as the reception goes, it was small, just the relatives.

I bought a suit in Lethbridge, a beautiful log cabin brown suit; of course they were wearing the skirts to the ankles in those days. I bought the hat, too, and I paid twenty-five dollars for it; in those days that was high. I was all in brown, and the hat had lovely, bright flowers on it, and a veil.

❦ I was at my aunt's place when I went to two weddings. One was in a hall and another in a thatched cottage. I was more Canadian, talked English; the others talked Ukrainian. All of a sudden crowds of people were going down to the spring with the bride and groom, and the violin playing. "Gee, what are they going to the spring for?" "Just an old custom," somebody said. That's all I got until I told my mother when I came home.

Then she explained to me about the customs of the old country. The matron of honor and the best man, or an older man or woman—not too old, but older—would go to the spring during the wedding, and the bride is supposed to give—well, at that time people didn't wear panties, but whatever it was, to show. My mother said in the old country, the girls used to be smart; if they'd had their period before, or else would use a chicken's blood if they did fool around with some of the boys.

A wedding marked the community's formalized approval of an event that had meaning for the whole society. The marriage itself was private. The relationship between a husband and a wife would evolve over the years. It became a structure built of many parts, including the economic circumstances facing a couple, their characters and dispositions, and their expectations of marriage, of themselves, and of each other. Some marriages worked well, satisfying both emotional needs and the urge for intimacy. Others caused women great bitterness and sorrow.

❦ We never had a scrap of any description. Of course he was the boss, and if he said anything I didn't dispute him. If I wanted to do it, I did it, and if I didn't I pleased myself about it. As I always told him, he thought he was the boss. No use arguing with a man if he thinks he's the boss.

❦ Her dad was against her. She was the one that picked her man, but he was a real boozer when he was young. She was sorry later on in years. She's still stuck with the same one; he's a little better now. These old guys have different ways and then you clash; settled in their ways. But then sometimes to settle an argument you shut up; you have to.

❦ My husband was kind of old-fashioned. He didn't even think a person should belong to women's clubs or anything like that. He thought there was too much pettiness in it. "Oh well," I said, "you can't be worrying about that all the time. You have to go for what you get out of it yourself." But I didn't join. I don't know why; he might have had something to do with it. But we just tried to consider each other's feelings.

My grandmother had come from a rich Irish family. She didn't love this man; it was a made-marriage. She said she had never kissed him before she married him. He brought her to the United States away from all she had. They settled on this farm and they were fortunate that she was among these Pennsylvania Dutch people. But she said as far as love went, there wasn't any there. She accepted his children but, the way she put it, "I cried a lap full of tears for twenty years." Every day for twenty years she cried a lap full of tears.

This English lady in the Peace country thought she was so superior. She had two little girls, and she was teaching them to speak in the English way, not with this horrible Canadian accent we have. I ran into her years later at Innisfail. There she could go to her own church, the Anglican, and she taught music. She wouldn't farm. Her husband bought a hog farm out of Innisfail and went back and forth from the farm to look after things. So I don't think she ever felt he was quite on the same level.

When the crops were good, my dad was generally in pretty good shape. He would take Mom for a walk, but the trouble was he would get her so worked up about how good things were going to be, and he always overestimated—because he wanted it all so badly—the bushels he was going to get. Mom faced that right then; she learned very soon to let him dream, but she knew that there still wasn't going to be enough money for a pair of sheets for the bed.

My husband was real rough. Sometimes he didn't talk. I dig whole garden up when he was uptown. He went all around there and I thought now he will come and tell me, "You have good job done and thanks for the job." He never said boo. His father was same; he said he was never like his father, but he was the same. I told him, "You worse than your father," and then he was so mad. Then he don't talk days to me. My husband was very hard to me.

He's more than eight years older than me. When we got married was the first night he was ever close to me. I didn't feel like getting married. I didn't even want to put on my clothes, didn't even curl my hair; nothing. I guess I looked so ugly when I got married. I didn't like it. I had to fight him for three nights before he can get close to me. I didn't want a man, until his sister came down and talked to me real good. I never did care for him. But when I had kids I cared for my kids. That's all I lived for is the kids. I didn't care for him; he can go out. He can do anything he wants. Comes home with women, I didn't care.

❧ You had to pretty well hang on in those days, no matter how bad it was. Having a roof over your head was better than nothing at all. There was plenty of fighting and quarreling, I can remember, and screaming and yelling. You can understand it, nerves and tension and all. But they realized that they had to maintain the home and if they broke up, the wife couldn't manage alone, the husband couldn't manage alone. I think they were all pretty tired and they didn't have much time to think about doing anything else but working and sleeping.

❧ I got married sixteen. Never went out with boys. Only saw him two times. Never been with another man, and he died nineteen years ago. Always alone; don't like nobody. I used to tell my husband, "As soon as I die I suppose you'll live with another woman," and he used to promise he'd never. Same with me. The priest calls me a nun! Just about! He was a good man. Never hit me, never.

❧ My parents were equal partners always. There was no feeling that women were inferior as far as our dad was concerned. There was stability and they gave us confidence and assurance, and of course there was confidence in God. They believed in God, they believed in His Son, they believed in the power of the Spirit. I think perhaps they taught us leadership for men, but they never made any difference between male and female otherwise. But they expected a man to take the lead. It didn't make the woman an inferior being as far as our family was concerned. God meant them to work together.

❧ My husband was a miner when we first got married, for about six months. He said, "I'd just as soon be a farmer." I'd rather have a little less money than see him go down that hole. You go down so deep and I couldn't stand seeing him come home being so tired. So I worked out with him for wages until we got on our own. We didn't have any children so he was my husband and baby. I kind of spoiled him a little. I wish he was here now.

❧ Out there on the farm we used to be up at five in the morning and sometimes went until twelve at night. When it was time to go in and get supper ready my husband used to say, "Take it easy. Rest a bit; I'll run in and get the kettle on."

He had half a mile to go to the house. By the time I got in the kettle was on and the supper was on and all we had to do was sit down and eat. He never said, "You do this," and I never said, "You do that." Fifty-seven years we worked together.

Working together: that was what it was all about. Women expected marriage to be a working partnership. It might provide them with love and intimacy, affection and warmth, loneliness and isolation, or anger and bitterness. All these were experienced as part of marriage. If frontier women expressed sincere devotion and loving loyalty to their husbands, some of them also cried "a lapful of tears." Certainly, intimacy was preferable to distance and loneliness. Love, however, was not what marriage meant. Before 1929, its primary purpose was not emotional. Rather, it was a working partnership designed for survival, productivity, and reproduction. The marriage of two people was the means for economic survival. Friendship might result from a couple's working together. Respect might unite them. However, deprivation, poverty, isolation, or downright meanness could make married life unpleasant, and even violent. Society and culture had deemed that a husband, as head of the unit, was in control and had to be obeyed. The lessons girls learned in their adolescence and during courtship taught them not that marriage would bring happiness or romance, but that marriage meant survival for themselves and the children they would have.

CONTRACEPTION
and
CHILDBIRTH

Marriage meant children. Women normally expected that babies would follow soon after the wedding. Whether the marriage was satisfying or not, the major source of women's identity in the frontier world lay in the children they bore and raised. A traditional means of defining women was by their function as mothers. What were women for? Quite clearly, one of the answers was that women were for having children. Women themselves accepted their procreative function as their first purpose, agreeing that giving birth and raising children validated their existence, more perhaps than their economic, creative, or political capacities. Raising children was in any case itself creative, and many of the political activities of women were undertaken to make better homes and families; they worked and produced for their families.

The women I talked with also provided evidence they sought some control over their bodies, their labor, and their lives. Many of them tried to limit the number of children they would have, attempting to give shape to one part of their lives. While social disapproval, medical mismanagement, or unpredictable fertility might defeat their attempts, family limitation was a major way for women to assert, even if only to themselves in a whisper, that they needed to define themselves not only as people who reproduced.

Discussions of birth control proceeded rather delicately. I came to believe that the inhibitions about the practice and discussion of contraception lay precisely in the subversive act of taking control. Women spoke discreetly and often with caution of their own or their neighbors' attempts at controlling births. Knowing that their actions defied not only acceptable standards, but also definitions of women, they were slow to discuss birth control.

Many women, in fact, knew very little about the subject, partly because abortion and contraception and even distributing information about them were illegal. Doctors were loathe to direct women toward family limitation; certainly single women, as far as I can discern, could not hope for their advice. Nevertheless, despite inadequate sources, women sought information from neighbors, relatives, magazines, and even from husbands, in the case of some women whose husbands brought from Europe knowledge about the condom. Women sought that information, though few of them found helpful answers and, like Elizabeth King, expressed frustration.

🌿 For my part, I think two [children] are enough. There wasn't any such thing then. It seems it was our lot. My grandmother had quite a funny saying. She used to say, "The good Lord taught us how to have children but he didn't tell us how not to have them."

The women who attempted "not to have them" used a variety of contraceptive methods, including the diaphragm, which they obtained with difficulty, prolonged nursing of babies, condoms, withdrawal, and abstinence.

🌿 Most of the people used the rhythm method. There was a diaphragm, too, and different jellies that were supposed to help. The doctors weren't supposed to tell you. One doctor would say, "There are methods that some doctors can give you," but he wasn't equipped to give it. After my son was born he told me, "This has got to be your last. I won't guarantee your life if you have another one." I read certain American magazines at the time. I read about different ways, this jelly, and some tablets, and some kind of ring. I wrote my cousin in the States and asked her about it, and she told me what to do. I went to this doctor in Calgary and he fitted me. I went to a drugstore in Calgary to buy a rubber diaphragm; no drugstore here in Canmore had those things. If I knew, probably lots of others knew, too, because there was an awful lot of people in town that only had a small family.

🌿 One family that only had two children, the woman wasn't too well, so they didn't have them. Another woman I knew when I was quite young nursed her baby until she was four years old so she wouldn't have another one. With me that wouldn't have worked at all.

❧ A family of seven children seemed unusual. I think there were a lot of Scottish people in our area, and it seems to me they're more restrained with the Presbyterian upbringing.

❧ There was no sex talk, no birth control talk, nothing. I never heard it. Maybe people asked their doctors. Also, the men knew more. The men knew what to do from the time they're kids. They talked about it. One friend of mine had only two sons. Of course, her husband wasn't very faithful to her, so maybe ...

❧ They didn't know any better. There was one lady that was well known, who wrote books—oh, Margaret Sanger. [A crusader for birth control.] I know my mother didn't want so many. Once she went to see a doctor who gave her some medicine to take, and she did lose the baby. The last baby she had was born dead. She nearly died with it, too. Myself, my health went between my second and third. Then we got smarter. Somebody sent some safes in the mail. I don't know who gave our name. We used them for a while, but I was ashamed to go and buy them in the drugstore.

Maternity home run by a midwife from England, Blairmore, 1913.

❦ We had our birth control: when we were out working, we didn't feel like having sex. We were too tired. You hear about families with thirteen children; that lady must not have gone to work.

❦ When I was ten there was another baby. In the meantime there was at least one miscarriage that I remember. I remember coming home from school, Mom being in bed, and the doctor being there. Mom never told us the facts of life in so many words, but rather in general conversation. We didn't learn it from animals because if anything like that was happening, my father wouldn't allow us round the barns. But Mom told it in telling her life story, and of course, having two older sisters, I learned a lot of it that way. But that time I seemed to know what had happened without being told. She was a person who didn't have regular periods, and she'd be three months pregnant and wouldn't know it. This made it very difficult for the old-fashioned method of birth control. Too, Father was opposed to birth control, and even at the times when he agreed, like to the French safe, I don't think he carried it out. He was a very sexual man. Well, what I'm saying is, he's still alive, and old!

You know, I think that for a lot of the women, sex was a mechanical thing, where they didn't look at it as we do now as a form of love. I think a woman looked at it as something that a husband had to have regardless of love or emotion, but also, if she was a strong-minded woman she could say no and not feel that she was depriving him. My husband's mother was a very poor English person. She had to get married; they had one child. Then when she came out here there was another, and another one two years later. From then on, he was locked out of her bedroom. Of course, she didn't like him anyway, so it made it easy. It was easy for women who hadn't built a real relationship.

This is why there were more unknown mistresses on the side. And with the rhythm system so unsafe, the women must have sensed that their husbands were going to a prostitute. There was no open prostitution in Calgary like in later years but, my goodness, the bank manager was having affairs and another old geezer was sitting in the show feeling every young woman's legs.

Back then, a man or woman could go through their whole life and not experience it, and not do them any harm. But now, in our modern day, you wouldn't dare admit you hadn't had an experience; you're looked on as pretty odd. I think that sex was not as important then.

Catholic women like Lily Dawes often agreed that contraception was not socially or religiously acceptable, yet she evinced a kind of stubbornness over the control of her body after having given birth to five children.

Cree mother and child, Innisfail, 1890s.

I was married twenty-five years; a man over in Lac La Biche asks me, "How many kids you got?" "Five." "Only five? You're not going to be saved." They had big families, twelve, fourteen over there. They didn't believe in preventing births. They'd say, "God never gave a sheep more wool than he can carry." But I said, "I'm the one raising the family. I'm not going to raise kids to get in trouble."

Many women had no idea of how to limit the size of their families.

We didn't really want so many children. But what could you do? They didn't do anything to prevent it them days. It was pretty hard to keep them, to clothe them and feed them, but we was lucky on the farm. We raised everything ourselves. We worked from morning to night, mind you, with a big family.

As an ironic contrast, hear Nancy Graves, a nurse from England, speak. She worked in the public schools of Calgary from 1920 until the 1960s, often in ethnic, working-class areas of the city.

No, as a public health nurse back then I never talked about these things with mothers. They'd go to the school doctor for that; she had an office in City Hall. Anyway, they didn't want to be bothered. That's what's wrong with most of these people; they didn't want to be bothered using contraception.

Abortion was also part of the spectrum of women's ways of limiting family size. Whether legal or illegal, women have always resorted to this method. Its illegality did not inhibit its use, although it increased its danger and intensified women's fear and guilt. Talk of contraception moved almost imperceptibly toward discussion of abortion as a necessary part of women's reproductive lives.

In my day, nobody knew much about birth control. It was just like a secret. You might get it in a book; I used to ask a nurse I knew what it was all about. All she told me was this rhythm method because she was a Catholic. So I tried to follow that. That ovulation I just couldn't understand. I was thirty-eight when I had change of life. I had six children. Some of the other Métis women knew more than me. I guess the priests didn't approve, but the women figured that's the Indian way, not the white man's way. They used a black bag from the bladder of a bear. They'd dry it, then mix it with some liquid, and then they'd lose the baby. There must be medicine in that. They figure that's okay. It's from the land and they figure it didn't do any harm. Well, the priest didn't know about it. Nobody told him about it.

🌿 My parents must have practiced some kind of contraception because my mother had seven children, two of whom died, but they were married when Mother was barely twenty. So there was a lot of time to have had more. Once I came across a condom in my father's vest pocket. In fact, ours was a larger family than most in the '20s, so people must have talked about it more than they'll admit. There was probably more abstinence too than there is now. And once, when I was about twelve, I went to a knitting class. I could hear two women talking about something, very hush-hush; one of them was saying to another, "She used a knitting needle." I remember thinking that the way they were talking would probably cease if they knew I was listening. I knew it was something adult.

🌿 This woman had done something to herself with a knitting needle. She'd had a miscarriage, but she was flowing and flowing. She got weaker and weaker. She got so weak you'd think she was wax. I said, "Tom, she's dying." I took a basin, washed her face, put a dress on her. We had to carry her to the car, where we put pillows. She nearly died in the hospital. They didn't have blood plasma like now. She was in the hospital two or three weeks. It wasn't the first time; I guess she had already done that before. She didn't have any more children after that. I think they used to watch, you know what I mean? When they had intercourse he would probably just take it out. That's the only way we were doing it, and I got so that my heart wasn't in it.

🌿 Some people got things from their doctor. They had tampons; I don't know what they were made of, but they had slippery elm bark and some other things in them. Or they'd take huge doses of Lydia Pinkham pills, and of course they had ergot. Doctors performed abortions, too. I know that they did, ever since I can remember. When I was in high school, about 1915, they used to go down to Great Falls, Montana. I remember a doctor friend of mine saying, "I wish to God I could close that clinic down there and start one here. The girls don't get proper care down there."

Most women did not seek to prevent all births. Certainly they wanted children at some time in their lives. Infants were welcomed joyfully by mothers, by families, and by communities. Yet the difficulties of conceiving and giving birth were dreaded, in part for their intrinsic travail and danger, and in part out of fears of the potential loss of the child. Millie

Melnyk's account of her hazardous pregnancies and deliveries was poignant; its terrible ending renders it even sadder.

In the night I woke. I was all wet. I didn't even know that your water breaks. I didn't tell my mother; just got up, changed the sheets. It didn't soak right through the mattress pad, and it was our own bed. The next day we went to a picnic; Monday I went out with a lady. We were collecting money for a women's magazine. But the pains didn't really get me till Thursday. My father was over. My husband used to read out loud to him, because he was just learning to read. I could hardly wait for my father to go home to bed. When he finally left, I knelt down, put a basin down. I'm flowing and I don't know what's the matter. Suddenly I'm so weak; Tom catches me and carries me onto the bed. Good thing he did; I didn't fall. He took a big towel, wet it and put it on my head, and then went up to get my mother. The first thing she says when she comes in the door was, "What did you do to yourself?" "Nothing." See, the women used to do things and she thought I had done something. I was so hurt that she should think that, and anyway this was supposed to be such a secret. In the meantime, Tom went for the doctor, who came and put me to sleep and took it out and fixed me. It's about six weeks that I was pregnant. My mother had it and she showed it to me; it was about like this, like a kitten. You can't tell yet what it would have been. I laid in the bed several days; my brother came to help me.

About six months after I was so weak, so pale. So weak I couldn't take the spoon to my mouth. I said to my auntie, "I'm so weak; I just can't." She told me not to take the medicine the doctor left me. We called a taxi. I could hardly walk to it. We went to our first doctor, the old doctor. I know then I broke down and told him I didn't mind that I was pregnant. "I would love a baby but I'm afraid that this baby will die too because I'm too weak and thin."

He gave me a tonic in a bottle. The tonic was just like wine, pinkish and it tasted very good. Before I had half the bottle I began to get stronger; by two bottles I was really strong, really healthy, and my daughter was born.

When that happened we were at a picnic. Some good friends were with us; one of them wasn't exactly a midwife, but people used to call her that. She was a very nice woman who had quite a lot of children, and she would often go with the doctor. At eight o'clock my pains came every eight minutes. It was a good thing that my neighbor had told me that when she had babies she would have diarrhea every fifteen minutes. It got me after twelve at night, and I was clean by eight o'clock in the morning. Then Tom went and got the doctor. The baby was right down there, but I didn't have any bearing. The doctor said, "Just bear down." I could feel the baby, right there, and I know I was crying. I said I was dying. The midwife said she'd never cried but "With you," she said, "I was crying because it was so difficult." The doctor would give me just a drop, now and then, of chloroform, which I hated. He didn't want to take the baby with an instrument. He began spreading me and trying to get that baby, but boy, was I torn. No stitches either. When he took that baby it was just like a rabbit, a skinned rabbit. They slapped her a few times across the back, and then the woman bathed it.

My husband walked all the way to Blairmore because he knew that everybody would contribute a shot of whiskey for this lady, the midwife; he knew she liked that. But it was a girl; he was disappointed. I knew he was disappointed because when he came back he said he was just going out, and I said, "Yes, because it was a girl." I wanted a girl, and he wanted a boy. I felt kind of

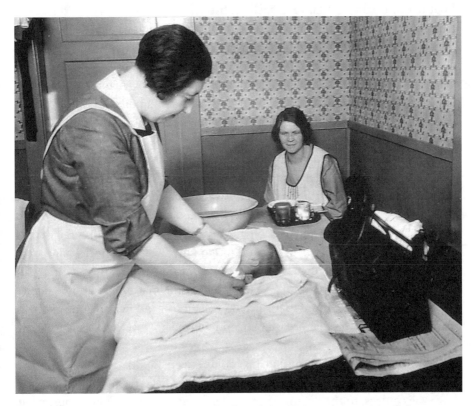

Member of Victorian Order of Nurses bathing baby during a home visit, Calgary, 1929.

hurt. The doctor came after and he said, "Do you still want to die?" And I said, "Yes." Every time I wanted to urinate I had to go on a pot, and it burned, without stitches or anything.

In the beginning she cried all night, all day. My husband would help me. He'd go night shift to work so he could help me as much as possible with the baby. I got very little sleep, and would work in between. The lady was very good. She came for two weeks. She was like a mother.

Tom said, "Never again that you'll have another baby." But I didn't know anything. I'll tell you how much we knew. He said to me, "If you don't enjoy at that time, if you don't want it, then you won't get pregnant." So he wouldn't help much with it. He enjoyed it but, you know, I never enjoyed it.

Then when she was five months old, I got pregnant again. I remember one evening my father stayed late at my house. He was so particular. He wanted his pants pressed, and even the coat sleeves. I was so tired and I pressed the sleeve, I suppose with a wet cloth, but the iron touched and burned it. I cried a lot about that. I used to get fainting spells at first. I was over at a very good friend's house when I didn't feel good. She said, "What's the matter? Are you … ?" You were even ashamed to say that you were pregnant. In fact, I didn't tell my mother and father until later. By this time the baby was on the bottle. The milk was too thick, and I had to pump my breasts. It was even too thick for the pump. I used cow's milk. I had to stir it until it was to a boil, and then I had to stir it until it got cool, so it wouldn't have that little skim on it, and then I'd dilute it with water.

We didn't have a carriage or anything. We put her on chairs with a pillow. I was very fussy though. That day she went she was nice and lively, holding her head up nicely and everything. That night we were in bed and she was crying; I was rocking her and Tom says, "Look, I'll take over. You go to sleep." So he rocked her and then he put her on the two chairs. But I didn't fall asleep because I'm like a mother hen. All of a sudden my husband put his hand over to the baby to pick her up. She was pinned into a little feather quilt I had made, sewed with the little puffs. I said, "What's the matter?" He said, "I don't know." She had a little bit of foam around her mouth and her eye, one eye, was open. We opened the blanket quickly and started to rub her legs. He knew some first aid.

I think she was still warm, but he couldn't seem to do anything. And her eye … I was petrified. I ran very quickly—it must have been a mile—up and down the coulees, to the doctor. He came back with me. I don't know just what he put down she died from, the chest or whatever. And so we had her one night in the house, and then we didn't have her anymore. That was my flesh and blood. I wanted her a lot.

We put her nicely dressed in a coffin. That night I didn't have much sleep. I went in the night to the baby and I felt her. I kissed her on the face. People were very good at the funeral. Everybody was very nice to me. Then they buried her.

The loss of her baby was also a great blow to Joanna Ricci. With tears in her eyes, she re-experienced her pain as keenly when telling me about it as she had fifty years earlier.

I didn't have children until four years after I was married. And then I lost the first baby. It was kind of a weak baby. It's really tough; you look forward to it, and then it's just like someone takes everything away from you. I thought, "Why me?" After you wait that long and then you lose it, it seems like all the

Family group, Calgary, 1912.

bottom went out of your world. I got so I hated babies after that. I'd see women with baby buggies and I'd turn the other way.

Women went to great lengths to save premature babies. With severely limited technology, one group of rural neighbors devised an ingenious way of saving a baby boy.

I can remember Homestead's little baby when he was born. He was only two pounds. Now what do you do with a premature baby back in those days? Well, this Mrs. Lind was a Swedish woman, and they lived about six miles from us. Mrs. Homestead was at her place when the baby arrived. They rolled him in oil, or maybe vaseline, and into a little white casing right up to his head. I can still see that little tiny head. They put him in a shoebox packed with blankets. Then they put him in the warming oven of the coal stove for an incubator, and kept the lid open for circulation of the air. Mom and Mrs. Lind took turns staying up at night and keeping the heat in the stove just right so that the baby's temperature wouldn't drop. They fed him with an eye-dropper. They

Family group, Lone Pine, 1910.

had him six weeks in that warming oven and Mrs. Lind didn't dare bake bread because the stove would get overheated. They built another oven outside with stones so they could save that one little baby. These two women working to save that little baby. And, by jingo, he's a great big six foot guy!

Women were attended sometimes by midwives, sometimes by physicians or husbands, and sometimes, in surely the most devastating metaphor for women's isolation, they lay alone to give birth.

The only time the Ukrainian women would call the doctor was when there was something serious. Mostly they had an older lady. The women would all come to visit you and bring fruit and cookies. When my mother had her last baby I was about twelve. I was mad she was having this baby because I had looked after the youngest boy. My dad brought this midwife but she didn't know anything; she didn't have any children. She thought the baby was coming head first, but it was coming with the knees. My mother suffered all day long; late in the evening the midwife said to my father, "I can't do anything; go for the doctor." The doctor got stuck quite a ways from the house and had to walk through the snow. He said to my father, "It's either your wife or your child." My father said, "The wife." My father was giving my mother the chloroform and the doctor and my uncle were pulling the baby out. I was holding the lamp. I was so sleepy I almost dropped it. The baby was so big. It was all swollen up. To me it looked about two or three months old. She had to wear a belt later on, in the lower parts.

My mother told me of this incident where a baby was born and the doctor had to break its arms and legs to deliver it because it was what you call a breech, and in the home with no facilities.

I was only married a year, and my first girl was born in the house, but we had a nurse. Mostly all of the colored people here in Amber Valley had this same midwife. She went north of us too, to the white people. She'd stay right in your house until nine days even, and cook and do the wash. Everybody just loved her.

My first baby I had at the hospital. It was a big boy. My husband was quite proud of him. One night we went to the show and he had him in his arms. A friend of his come up and said, "What have you got there?" "A big ten pound boy," he says.

I had one that was thirteen pounds. All the others I had on the farm, on my own, though sometimes with a nurse. It's a funny thing: I never thought of anything being the matter with babies, and I had no troubles, out of all thirteen kids. Most of them are six feet, too.

The second one, my husband delivered; I mean, he was there when the baby was born. The nurse was afraid to come because she had the flu. The man that went to get her went to look for another lady, but my husband said, "No reason; the baby is here now." They had quite a laugh about it. The third boy was born all by myself. When my husband went to look for somebody, the baby came a little sooner than I figured out. The doctor came after the thirteen pound one, and he said, "You are the luckiest woman I ever saw. I got babies out in the country three months old that are not as big as this one." He couldn't get over it. He thought I'd be tore to pieces with a big baby like that.

Women had mixed feelings about hospital births. Some of them saw a stay in a hospital as a sort of holiday from household chores. Others associated it with illness, an experience that conflicted with their view of childbirth as a natural event. Others found the maternity home a sort of compromise. These homes were private houses owned and run by women, some of whom were nurses, who took in women for the birth and for ten days to a fortnight after. They helped the physician attend the birth and then looked after the mother's and the infant's needs. Running the maternity homes, which were found in rural and urban areas, was one of the few means of earning a living restricted to women. The women who had had their children there spoke very warmly of the homes and the nurse-midwives who lovingly and caringly ran them. Still other women returned to their families in eastern Canada for several months, and one even went back to England to give birth.

The oldest was born in the hospital in Calgary. That would be 1910. The ambulance was just a team of horses. Once in the hospital was enough for me. I didn't like it. I had never seen a nurse, and you didn't get doctors' visits before the baby was born. That was my first time to see the inside of a hospital. Drove me crazy.

I was all right, and my girl was born. But there was a young girl in the same room with me and she started to feel bad. So I didn't sleep any that night. She cried all next day with her pains. The nurse would just tell her she couldn't do anything for her; kind of short about it. And this girl's husband was way up north. He had no way to come and see her. It got worse toward evenings and

Couple from Scotland with their child, Coleman, 1905.

they took her finally to the case room, about midnight. So I never slept that night; that was the second night. At that time they kept you in hospital fourteen days. They didn't even let you sit up until the eleventh day.

When my husband took me out of the hospital he had to hire a livery team to take me out, and then we took the train back home, and after that I had to travel ten miles in the wagon, with a little baby. All my others were born at home.

The first two were born in the hospital, the old General in Calgary. I had twins down there, but I lost the boy; never brought him home. When he was born the doctor says, "Well, your boy is fine, but I'll not give you much for your girl." And I've still got her. I put it down to that they didn't bring him often enough to nurse. I told the doctor so. I said, "That baby isn't getting any nourishment. I have to squeeze it into his mouth. He hasn't got the power to nurse." He got weaker and weaker. That was a blow because he was such a nice baby, and a boy.

There weren't near as many had them at home as in the hospital. The majority came there. Some of them came because it was a rest for them. They'd stay ten days in those times. One lady, every year she was in. "Well," she said, "I came for a holiday."

I was born in England. There were no doctors out here, so my grandfather sent the money out and told Mother to come home. The family were worried about the delivery's being out here, so Mother had the Queen's physician to take care of her. I was over there until I was six months old.

The midwives with whom I spoke were warm women who viewed their role as one of assistance and support to the mothers. They saw birth as a notable life event for these women, one that they felt privileged to share.

Fifty-three babies I deliver. The first time I was sixteen; that man he come and get my mother. I went with her. I caught a baby girl. If trouble, send to a hospital. There's one woman ask me now —I'm ninety-one—but I says I can't do it. I'm too old.

My dad, you see, delivered all the women out here. As I grew up, I always helped him. I learned with him. He had learned first from midwives in the States, and had instructions when we came out here. He had a book from a doctor in Morinville, too. After I took over, I always had a good book too, and followed the instructions. I had all my equipment in my satchel, and my nice white uniforms. I'd have them ready for the next time. Sometimes I'd bring the babies home with me, and then my husband would bring me to the mother for nursing time. I'd fix them up there, give them their bath, fix their beds, and then I'd come back home.

My own first baby was born when I was a few days from my sixteenth birthday. A ten-and-a-half pound baby. My second baby was twelve pounds. It was my dad that was my doctor. It was a big baby, but my dad was so good. He gave the time and the help.

When I was helping the doctor the first time he came down—I was helping with the cleaning in the house—and said, "The lady upstairs she's feeling sick and is going to have the baby, but my nurse is sick." Well," I said, "I ain't a nurse, though I wanted to be, but if I can help you, I'll come up and help." So I washed and put on a clean apron and went upstairs and helped him with this baby when it was born. But he made me mad! I didn't know that you slap their bottoms to make them cry. He slapped the baby's bottom and I punched him in the back! I laughed so much afterwards and hugged him and asked him to forgive me. I just didn't know.

Well, I brought twenty-six babies into the world, all on my own with no doctor. It's given me such a gorgeous feeling. I wanted to be a nurse, and I wanted to be where little children was. I loved the kids, but I didn't know I couldn't have any children. So I gave all my love to all the kids.

THE HOUSEHOLD
WORLD of WOMEN

There is an old saying about the west being a fine place for men and dogs but hell on women and horses. When travelers or western residents said that, they usually meant that women were isolated in rural homesteads where the hard work and drudgery were unrelieved by socializing. I think that women perceived their work differently. They worked hard, in city homes or farm houses. Their days went on endlessly, leaving them with little extra time, leisure, energy, or inner resources. "We did the laundry, we did the milking, we made butter, we made soap, we killed, we cured, we canned. It was one persistent thing after another." The routine may have seemed like hell to observers, but the women themselves saw the work as something they had to do. "Well, you just had to keep going." Over and over I heard them say that. They had no choice, they felt. Most of them had come west because of someone else's decision; the move was not of their own making. Nor was what they found here under anyone's control: the land was too dry or too wet, the forest too dense or the vista too bare. The best they could do was accommodate necessity by providing their labor, often unvalued, for the family's survival.

Women continued working day after day, night after night, because their work was imperative. They could not make a decision to move on, to go back, or to quit; mostly they could only look over the situation in which they found themselves and do what was necessary. Pride might emerge from persisting, especially later in life when the work became a bit easier, but for most women, through much of their lives, the family's existence demanded that they keep going.

That may have been perceived as hell by some; many others thought it was the only possible accommodation. It wasn't good; it wasn't bad. Work was just something they had to do. It was not glorified by the rewards of the marketplace, by social approval, or by an ethic of work; nor, by contrast, was it degraded by the mythology about ladies of leisure. Work was just what one had to do. The work that went on and on, draining, repetitive, and consuming, did not leave much to nourish the spirit, feed the imagination, or nurture creativity. Work was sheer and simple necessity. It did not inspire poetry or folk tales, or create mythic heroines. Women just worked unremittingly day after day, season after season, at something "you just had to do."

At Morinville it was a large house, in the old and very rough way. One day I came out of my bedroom to my mother with a handful of bugs, asking her what they were. We found out from neighbors that they were bed bugs. Then the war on bed bugs started. We used creeping powder, hot water, and lye—anything to get rid of them. We sold that place and moved to another farm. It was the same thing over there. Mother started the war on bed bugs again.

Maria Borisenko came from Ukraine to a wooded homestead in 1909. Her husband worked in lumber camps during the winter and on wealthier homesteads in the summer. One month of each year he could work on his own place, clearing an acre or two. His wife stayed on the homestead to tend the children and the few animals—seven years, in fact, without ever leaving the place. She wept as she recalled the hard work, the isolation, and the deprivation of those early years.

Nobody here do embroidery; no time, couldn't afford the thread. I learned already cross stitch in the old country, but my mother say I'll never eat bread if I embroider. No money; salt bacon and smoke it because no money for jars.

Economic status—poverty for many, of course—influenced the kind of work that women did. The poorer they were, the more they had to do, like Millie Melnyk in the following excerpt, and Viola Carter's aunt in the one after.

I'll tell you how we did, we women. My mother and father never bought coal at all. The women went to the dump. They used to put coal in the cars.

All that coal went into different railroad cars, and then there would be coal in between, sometimes lovely coal, big chunks you could cut with the axe we had in the house. This place we used to call the dump, where they moved the coal in chutes, was about a mile from our house. The coal would fall down into the coulee; some of the men were good and would give you a little chance, moving the coal slowly. You'd go down the coulee and pick it up quickly—not all of it, because some of it was burning and you'd have to watch that. From there it would be quite a ways that you'd have to bring it up to put in a pile. Then my father would come after work with a barrel on a cart to bring it home. We'd all have an apron to carry it in; my sister who was so small and thin, one large chunk, and I'd have three or four, and Mother more. We knew which was bone and which was the coal, slippery and so beautiful.

I did that right through until I started to go to work. We were never out of coal; sometimes I would take a great handful of coal dust, run it through my hands. Even after we were all older, my mother went for coal. I felt so sorry for my sister; she was so small and thin. And there were great big bugs from the coal that bit you. Everybody knew us when we came from Hardieville. We always smelled like smoke because the dump burned all the time. We didn't notice until we got to town, when we noticed how the others knew we were from Hardieville. The smoke got into everything.

❧ My aunt had nine children. The spring was down below; they had to carry the water in buckets to the house, and it was uphill. For a family like that it meant a lot of walking. The worst thing of all was the flies. The barn was way down—my uncle had put it there on purpose—but these blessed flies came from somewhere. We used to tie willow rods, every kid in the family, open the doors, and shush these flies out. There'd be a black swarm of them. They used to drive my aunt crazy. Years later they had fly paper all over the place, in corners, everywhere.

Things got a little better, and she was able to drive to town when she finally got a horse and buggy. All those years up to that time I can never remember her going to town or anywhere else. She used to make about nine loaves of bread a day, every day of her life. It was set the night before, and raised all night. In winter, she'd wrap it in blankets to keep it from freezing. They had no way of keeping the house warm, just the big pot-bellied stoves after a while, which they'd fill full of green wood and it would hold pretty well all night . She was too busy to go out. She had sewing to do, and all this cooking, and mending, just everything. I've often thought about it. It's a wonder she kept her sanity.

They had come here from the east with very little money. They filed on a claim, and were able to buy a horse, but they couldn't build a house because they hadn't any funds. There didn't seem to be much time around either. Unfortunately, they went into a worse part of the province. The soil was bad there, still is. Their first house was a sod house. I think they learned how to build it from a neighbor, a Russian chap. It was twelve feet by twenty feet for the five of them. They lived there for two years. I remember now with amazement her telling stories of the garter snakes who would winter in the roof, up into the sods where the heat was. It wasn't unusual for a garter snake to stick its head down.

When she came up, everything had to be done by hand. There wasn't even a store where they could buy clothes. They even had to grind their cereal for breakfast. I loved it as a kid: brown and kind of crunchy. She had a great big black pot, three gallons, maybe five, a round-bottomed pot that could sit down in the stove. In the morning she cooked the cereal in it. It always disappeared. Then for the evening meal she'd cook the stew in it. They practically lived on beans because they had little or no meat. Any cattle they had they couldn't afford to kill, but had to keep for milk and cream.

They didn't have a separator yet. Instead, they used big pans, like a dish pan, two and a half or three feet across. They'd fill them half full, and then she skimmed the cream off into big cans, ready for shipment. In winter, she used to put it out in a snowbank, in summertime, in a spring. About twice a day, she'd skim the cream off. A little money came in that way.

Eventually they built a log house, a lovely place. It was about fifty feet long, and maybe twenty-five wide. They had one huge room upstairs over the living room and dining room. By this time, she had seven kids.

She used to bring us vegetables, which we'd store in the cellar, eight or ten feet underground: potatoes, turnips, cabbage, carrots. I never remember green beans, and I never knew what broccoli was. Imagine living like that!

The children, of course, were not exempt from laboring for the family's subsistence. Many women, like Patricia Pound, expressed a preference for outdoor work in their youth, resisting perhaps the unremitting household work that awaited them as adults.

We were a family of nine. As the years went on, the boys were out on their own, so the girls were the boys really. We used to take turns at chores. Some stayed in the house and done the housework, and some went out to milk fourteen cows and separate the cream by hand. As a kid I hated housework and wanted to be outside, but my sister was good at sewing and housekeeping, so I used to do her work outside if she'd do mine inside. Every once in a while Mother'd put a stop to that. "Some day, my lady, you're going to want to know how to cook." I didn't think that time would ever come!

That time did come. Learning to bake bread symbolized for the women their mastery of women's work. Many women recalled baking with more warmth and enthusiasm than they felt for any of their other work. It may have been the tangible reward of the job that made it appealing; it may also have represented the essence of women's work with the family.

🌿 Myself, in the beginning, I didn't know how to boil water. My husband got a hundred pounds of flour. I'd bake a batch of bread; it would be just like a rock, and I'd throw it over the hill. The next day, I'd start another batch of bread, and throw it over the hill. I used a hundred pounds of flour and threw it all in the thick woods. Finally, I got so that we could eat it. But we couldn't eat it at all for the first hundred pounds.

🌿 I was the third in a family of six girls and three boys. As each of the girls got through high school they got a time at home helping Mother. I was kind of in between, so I didn't get that chance. I never had the slightest idea about baking bread. When I came out here to join my husband, he had the name of being the best bread baker in the district. I knew I'd have to do it sometime, but I thought I'd let him bake the first batch. Now, I don't know whether it was by design or whether it just happened that way, but that bread was so hard you couldn't break it by throwing it against the wall! So I thought, "If that's what you call good bread, I'll have a try at it myself." I had various results for years, not often very satisfactory, until I came across a recipe for brown sugar bread. You mixed it up at night, and in the morning the bread would be over the side of the five gallon crock. From then on I had very good bread.

Baking bread was one household activity that linked frontier women to a collective memory of centuries of other women. The work became more meaningful when they could locate their work in the traditions of women. Fidelity to the customs of the lands left behind also provided a sense of continuity and pride to women like Jean Davis. From England, Jean derived social meaning by placing herself and her work within that tradition. All her life she identified with her English roots.

101

Always I cooked in the English way. We had our meat puddings like we used to have in England. People out here never heard of them; they thought they were meat pies. You rolled your dough and put it in a bowl. Then you cut up your meat and your onions, and put in a cup of water, salt, and pepper, then the pastry on top, then put a cloth over the top and tied it tight. Then you'd boil it for three hours, took the cloth off carefully so you didn't pull the top of your pudding away, and had a gorgeous dinner. I still make my Christmas puddings. I don't care that people say it's too much work. Without a Christmas pudding, it's not Christmas.

Daphne Toll's people also came from England, bringing with them the army custom of the batman, which they maintained here. The family had a long history of association with the military. Her father and mother came to the North-West Mounted Police fort in the 1890s, raising their children at Fort Macleod and other forts farther north. Being part of an institution like the army clearly ameliorated the isolation of frontier life as well as the women's physical toil. Daily life was perhaps a bit less demanding for Daphne Toll's mother, an officer's wife, than it was for women who had to do their work unaided except by children.

Woman reading in her parlor, Calgary, c. 1912.

In those days, in Fort Macleod in 1898, we didn't have maids at all. We all had our own servant, a batman. They cleaned the boots and brought in the coal and wood. Sometimes a prisoner would do the work for us too. They did the garden. The Indians used to carry a round ball of iron on a chain attached to their feet so they couldn't run away.

> Middle-class urban women had household help too. Sometimes that help released them to volunteer activities, to greater leisure, and occasionally to paid work. The Jewish urban women I talked to almost invariably had domestic help, as they tended to be heavily involved in family businesses. The women who were themselves domestics bemoaned the low pay and hard work, but also saw the experience as a way of learning to do things "in a new way," different from their mothers' ways.

Mother had household help a lot of the time. You used to bring out girls from the old country, Scottish and Irish girls mostly. Some organization in the east sponsored it. You paid their fare out and then they worked it out for you. As a rule, they were a very nice class of girls. Probably too many in the family at home; they'd decided to see if they could better themselves out here.

When I was little we had the seamstress come in; naturally I wanted to sew when she was there. I was given scraps of fabric to make things for my dolls. She often used to take four or five little girls and help us with our embroidery; we'd have lemonade and cookies and be girls together. I'm the only one that's left.

When you got married your life changed. We'd go to parties because we had help, but you wouldn't tear off to the ranch every other day. You settled down to business. I had one person working for me; she did the cooking and the cleaning. Some girls were trained, and some I'd have to teach; some were city girls and some were country girls, though not immigrants by 1926.

> Some of the work was so clearly defined as "women's work" that there is very little evidence that husbands ever did it. Few women resisted doing "women's work," and also performed chores that, in more traditional or less labor-short societies, might not be thought appropriate to women. Very often, husbands imposed definitions of the appropriate and the inappropriate in realms that were not so clear cut. Gardening, for instance was defined differently, as women's or as men's work. Lizzie Helm said, "The

boys and Father wouldn't let me work in the garden. He said, 'Your mother didn't do it and you're not going to do it. It's no place for a woman.' Some of the others said that they wished their husbands were like that!" Anne Way was not to extend her labors to the garden either. "I didn't believe in doing the outside work. Roy didn't like it. Just nobody in New Brunswick ever did that work outside. I was never expected to do it." Estelle Nash's husband, on the other hand, deemed gardening appropriate for her—until he tried it. "For so many years I hoed potatoes; didn't think anything of it. Then one day my husband went out and hoed potatoes, and found out what hard work it was. That very day he got into the car, went out, and bought a tiller."

The most demanding season for rural women was threshing time. If their husbands hired large crews to bring in the harvest, they had to cook for the men, who apparently had gargantuan appetites. If they couldn't afford many hands, the wife worked in the fields and cooked too—all this along with the usual child care, washing, mending, and cleaning. Men dropped into their beds at night; women stayed up to finish the day's chores, preparing for the next day, and mixing and kneading vast quantities of bread.

Yet, threshing time was a season of excitement, especially if the harvest was good. It was the season that marked the passage of time in the most meaningful way, by visible achievements. It was also the moment that came closest to being a period of shared communal activity. Women often helped in each other's kitchens, sharing the burdens and the laughter. Large numbers of people congregated around the farms, sometimes neighbors and sometimes strangers who circulated praise for a woman's cooking. The audience for women's activities suddenly became larger than just the family. Women became, for a brief period of the year, part of a wider and sometimes more appreciative community. Thoughts of threshing time brought memories of shared activities to Marjorie Nester.

The women used to compete with each other for who would serve the fanciest spread. The men would go out on the threshing crews and they'd say, "Oh boy, can that woman cook! Boy, we had this and we had that." And, of course, the women were all interested. They'd ask, "What did you have at Brown's place, or Smith's place?"

One place my husband went the woman cooked stew every day. They threshed there for quite a few days. Stew, every day. They got quite sick of stew.

As they were about to move onto the next place, the next farmer asked, "Well, what do your men like to eat?" "Stew," he said. "They love stew." So they went to the next place, and she cooked stew!

One place, he told me, the mother and all the girls would stand behind the men: "Have some more chicken, have some more milk, have some more bread." They said they never saw anybody cook for threshers the way that family did.

> At ninety-eight, Bernice White's recollection of harvest time was vivid—its exhaustion, but its achievement, too, measured by empty barrels and flour bags.

I had a thirty gallon crock. I'd cut all the fat off a pig, cut it into big pieces according to what I wanted, and then put a brine over it. I sent down to Chicago for that brine. Every now and again I'd turn it around. When you'd had threshers for several days, the pork went down. You'd put up a twenty pound roast, and it'd be gone. You had to make a lot of other things besides; I used to can a lot of white beans. You'd soak them and cook them with bacon,

Sawing wood, Alderson, 1914.

in the oven, with tomato stuff. I'd put them into sealers so you could open them on the day you needed them. I've often wondered with amazement at the day I first saw a gang of threshers. Not only had I never cooked for them; I'd never even seen them before. There were nineteen men there that first time. Pies, pies would disappear. Breakfast by six: porridge and fried potatoes and bacon and eggs. A loaf of bread wouldn't go anywhere. And the cows to milk, and the chickens, and the children. Sometimes I had a young girl do the washing-up for me. As soon as we'd empty the plates she'd wash them up and get them ready for the next meal. I didn't have time to eat. And I didn't want to eat. I was too buoyed up. I'd fall on the bed at night just dead.

Cattle ranching made similar demands on women, but for longer periods of time, as Gail Richards recalled.

My husband had about eighty-five head of horses. Sunday was round-up day for them, and for the men. They'd try riding the bucking horses. By noon there'd be men on the corral fence sitting around watching. I would count the heads on the fences, then ring the bell—I had a cow bell he brought from Montana in 1910—and he'd tell them, "Come on, it's dinner time." Didn't matter if he knew them or not.

The spring after we was married there was no land broke, nothing but prairie grass. It was such a dry spring there was no hay up here at Strathmore, so somebody told him it was good hay down there by Chimney Hill. That's where Standard is now. A whole bunch of men went down there. My husband got two or three extra men and loaded up three or four wagons, one with oats for the horses. We had two big tents and seven men. We couldn't take beds. We mowed some hay when we got there and he put a tarp over it, put it over in the corner, and that was our bed.

I had nine to cook for there, with just the old stove with the firebox burned through into the oven. New married and pregnant. But I didn't think twice about it. I could make bread when I was so little I had to stand on an apple box to reach the table. The only thing I used to hate was whenever it would come rain when we was camped down there with three or four different outfits putting up hay. Whenever it was rainy and they couldn't hay, they would come sit in our tent and I had to cook, trying to get around all those men. They used to say that they were going to Peace River, and I used to wish they'd go right then, because it was hard to do in a tent with all those men. No women; I never seen a woman. I was down there two months and I never seen another woman.

The growing, buying, preservation, and preparation of food were women's responsibilities. They usually brought with them to the frontier a tradition of cooking learned from their mothers. Much of that was soon abandoned, except on ceremonial occasions and holidays, because the land, the storage facilities, and the time they had available were different from their mothers'. Ukrainians, Irish, Germans—the foods they served all came to resemble one another's, especially in the rural areas. Only a few maintained old traditions such as baked beans and brown bread; only a few sought escape from the probably adequate but bland regime.

We'd have porridge for breakfast, like kids today have cornflakes. When we were kids I'll bet you there wasn't one meal that we didn't have milk. For dessert at night we used to have pie once in a while, or rice pudding, baked apple, or pudding. My mother used to have the coffee pot on the back of the stove. Every time she felt kind of dry she'd have a cup of coffee.

They used to save carrots and rutabagas from the garden for winter. But they didn't do much canning of vegetables. My mother canned a lot of fruit; peaches and pears. After I got married, we started to can vegetables, and meat, too. We cured the pork. We had no other way of keeping it. We had an ice box later. You had to watch it that it didn't run all over the floor. It would drain into a pan. But that was better than nothing. You could keep your food for a little while; it was better than nothing. Was that a thrill, when we finally got a fridge!

The bread happened to be just awful because the flour wasn't any good. We lived more on this corn stuff, a corn meal that you would put with boiling water, let it come to a good boil, and put a bit of salt and a bit of butter. Then you'd pour it into a stick made of a branch, about an inch and a half around and all the bark taken off white as white could be and sanded. You'd press a spoon down on the corn stuff, leave it in the oven a little, and then just flip it out on a plate. That was good with everything, soups or anything.

We cured our own bacon. First you rub the salt real well into the back of the pig. Every two days you would rub that salt in and add some more; then the third week you'd take that off and rub some brown sugar mixed with salt real good into it. Then, about another week later, you'd hang that up. Your rolled oats and flour came in bags; well, you'd put the whole side of the bacon in that bag and hang it in your basement. Then you'd go and slice off whatever you needed, covering that with brown paper to keep the flies off. Everything you had for your table—butter, milk, sugar—you covered. We were really bothered with flies.

We bought flour and sugar and molasses and fruit. The molasses was for baking—ginger snaps—and for the baked beans and the brown bread. We used to have that nearly every weekend in the winter, still do. It was an eastern custom. I used to go east with Mother in the summer, to Prince Edward Island, her old home. The beans were done on Saturday, while all the work of getting ready for Sunday was being done.

I came out here a person who was used to fresh meat, fresh milk, fresh butter. All I had here was canned stuff; eggs maybe one month old. Oh, I was desperate, so I talked my husband into letting me have a few hens so we could have fresh eggs. Later, we could have a fresh chicken once a week. Then I talked him into getting me a wild cow; bought one from a chap down the river and I trained her to be milked, and we had fresh milk and cream. Then, when the bird season opened, we'd have those and fish—grayling are delicious to eat. In the winter there was moose and deer meat. As soon as I could, I put in a vegetable garden.

In the twenties, I went with my husband when he went to visit the irrigation stations. The women would frequently assemble in the house of the station owners, and I would talk to the women on nutrition. Some of the farm women had done some reading and would make comments. The majority of them just sat; took it as a form of entertainment. I was trying to give them a fundamental knowledge of nutrition so they could feed their families better. Generally, they ate white bread, even though they had all this nice wheat around. I would demonstrate one of the individual grinding mills, and a good many of those people around the country did buy them and ground their own wheat. Many of the farmers never raised vegetables on their little tracts of land. Some of them had no water and just couldn't raise them, but with a little encouragement they were able to get some water. A good many of those women had beautiful flower gardens, when they had access to some water that they could pour on the flowers.

In cities and towns, where stores were easily accessible, shopping was women's work. In the country, though, men most often did it because of weather, or roads, or because women could not be spared from the house for even a day, let alone for the two or three sometimes necessary to get to town and back.

❦ Mostly the husbands went for shopping because of the kind of roads; just trails they were, very poor driving. Only once in a while would a wife venture to go and take her children. It was a three-day trip, what's an hour's trip now. They'd come in the first day, rest the horses, and look around a bit. The next day they'd shop, and the third day they'd start back.

❦ Invariably, if there was a trip to be made to town, there was business to be done, or purchasing, so the men had to do it. The men were very much the head of the house. They used to angle across the prairie trails and down through Nose Creek and across the Langevin Bridge, which took you right through the house of ill fame area. That was the only way to get into Calgary. We only went to town once a week. Fact is, there were weeks on end when the womenfolk didn't get in.

❦ The farmers got together. Each week one farmer would go for the supplies; another week another one would go. It was such a long trip. They'd stay overnight at Alsask and come back the next day.

❦ We had to go to Athabasca for provisions in the winter, because in summer the roads were not very good; muskeg and swamp and fallen trees on the road. If you didn't have an axe you couldn't pass. We would both go for supplies with the small child who wasn't in school because I had things I wanted to buy.

The houses that provided the settings for and the source of women's labor were uncomfortable, distressing places for many of them, especially in the early years. Tents or sod houses with dirt floors, frame houses with bed bugs, inadequate water supplies, cramped quarters, and poor construction that could not keep out the cold or the wet—all these seemed to conspire against women. Here was the end of the road for them—it would be home forever—so they each attempted to make it feel like home. In part they were making do; in large part they were expressing their desire for a place, a place of their own different from any other, a place to call home.

❦ There were some sod houses and some log houses. When I first saw that long sod house standing there I thought, "What is that?" I thought it was a forest of some kind. We took that down and had a nice little house, very nice. We always planted flowers there. It was hard to get them to look nice because we had a hard-water well, and they needed soft water, so my husband used to go to a neighbor and haul water for washing and to put on the flowers. In the

Laundry day on a farm near Bon Accord, c. 1918.

spring the sloughs filled up, sometimes water standing there right up to summer, so then I had water. We always had a good crop of raspberries up there. The neighbor ladies came up, and we had a wonderful time picking them and making jam.

🌿 We lived in the tent until Christmas, 1912. Folks had assured us that Calgary didn't have cold weather before Christmas. Well, before the end of September the snow was up to the roof of the tent. Did we ever feel like fools! Mother cooked on a pail with holes punched in it. She had a very good friend there who was a gopher. He would come around and pick up all the stuff that she had dropped: the carbon, the peels, and then he'd go and eat my brother's breakfast. My brother didn't like the gopher, though Mother was very friendly with it, so there was a rift in the family for a while.

Later, when I taught, I learned about different kinds of architecture. Nearly all the Russians in the area had two houses. I called them the Sunday house and the Monday house. The Monday house was the kitchen, and the Sunday house was the bedroom. That one was always immaculately clean, though the other wasn't. Often, the oven was outside. The inside oven would be extended in clay and the whole family would lie on top of the clay. I was very shocked, easily perturbed. "I don't think that's decent," I said. My landlord said, "Well, it's a lot more decent that some of the things that go on in the east."

🌿 Father got a homestead next to my grandfather's out there by Three Hills. He and Mother moved out in the fall; they had nothing but this little shack, and Dad said he knew it was cold. He'd heard about the cold winters, so he went around collecting all the five gallon oil cans he could find. He scoured the prairie around and found them, left by the big outfits ploughing up virgin land, and opened them up and nailed them on the outside of the shack to try to keep the place a little warmer. He knew what the winter was going to be like. That was '06 and '07, which you may have heard was probably the coldest winter in Alberta. I can remember Mother saying that every morning when she got up, the nails on the inside of the shack would be covered with frost.

The house was very tiny, but there was a dining room and a living room combined, and how we got so many relatives in that room for a meal I'll never know, except that Mother had a table arrangement that would fold up against the wall. It would make room to seat people when she folded that up. The place would be bursting at the seams with relatives from Calgary in summer.

𝔴 Mother didn't mind the sod house. The only trouble we had was when it rained. It never stopped the rain. We used to sit with umbrellas over us. Course, it didn't rain often. There was only about two or three good crops while I was down there, ten years maybe. Otherwise you'd maybe get your seed back and that's all. Mostly there was the wild waving prairie grass.

𝔴 We first lived in the old sod house. It had a beautiful bay window. Mother could grow plants in that bay window; you never seen anything like it. Dad made the house. He took the walking plow and plowed furrows, and then they were cut into bricks about a foot wide this way and eighteen inches that way. With the walking plow you could get about four inch thicknesses of turf. Then he packed all that sod and laid it just like you'd lay a brick house. So we had about that much thickness in the walls. He cut poplar trees and put them on the inside of that, and against those he put the building paper so as to keep the dirt from falling in. That was tar paper for dampness and the white wallpaper in front of that for cleanliness and good looks. Partitions were made with the poplars, and the white paper tacked to them.

Mother and daughters and the cook car, Milo area, 1913.

The floor was hard as a rock because of walking on it, that dirt floor. Mother used to take a damp broom and sweep it all. We had very little dust. We lived in that for six years. I was too small to remember it, except you know how you get a mental picture of these things, because I was about six years old when we moved out of the sod house. We lived in it for six years. I was born there, and so was my baby sister. I'd say, "What are we?" and Dad would answer, "You're gophers because you were born under the ground." Well, it was a case of existence.

I can remember the log shack in Athabasca. I wasn't too old then, about six. One summer it rained for fifty-two days straight. This log cabin had just a mud roof and it was raining inside as well as outside. The only dry place there was was over the one bed; the rest of us slept on the floor because we didn't have beds. It was hard times. I remember Mom took the oilcloth off the big table and nailed it to the roof. That's the only place it was halfways dry in there. The rest of it was soaking wet.

We lived in the tent with the floor for several weeks, until Father finished the log house. Thirty by twenty-eight; that was a large house for then. He got the house up with a flat sod roof before winter set in. We lived in the whole house for the first few weeks until it turned cold. Then we lived in half the house; that got too cold, so they curtained off a quarter of the house. We pulled in the bed and pulled out the table at night.

The next year we were still living in this house. We still had the flat roof but by then we had a floor in the big bedroom, a room curtained off by poles with a nice rug pinned to the poles. Everybody kept stumbling on the poles. We were so proud of the rug in the bedroom; thought it looked really nice. My sister arrived then, from Ontario. She thought it was terrible. The rain was dripping through the flat roof. She was just through Normal School, and she said, "You know, nobody is expected to live like this. I'm going back on the first stage that goes out." But by the time she was there for two or three days she was used to it, and she never went back to Ontario.

There was one window and two beds in the house. They were against the wall; it was all ground where the beds were. Mother used to make mattresses out of straw and we slept—how many of us?—five or six on one bed, lengthwise because there was no room the other way. Mom and Dad slept on the other bed. To wash that ground floor all we did was took some dirt and water and made it thin, and then took a broom and swept with that dirt to wash away the dust. The kitchen was wood floor, boards. The dirt was easier to clean; for the wood you had to have a scrubbing brush and soap.

There was only two rooms, the dirt floor and the wood floor. They put up that thin paper because they couldn't afford the heavy tar paper. It hailed and made holes, and when the wind came it tore the paper off, and rained in. So Mother took my brother—Joe was small yet—on the quilt, put it under the table, and that's where he slept because it was raining into the house. It was dry under the table. After it stopped raining a bit, they couldn't stay no more in the house because it was leaking all over, so they went to the neighbor's house, not far so they walked. My mother said she got there and she couldn't sleep, because they had bed bugs. Till morning they stayed, and then she had to plaster everything at home again.

It wasn't whitewash; we couldn't afford whitewash, so she used ashes of a white poplar. In the old country I guess she learned it. She mixed the white poplar ashes with water, but sifted it first so all the fine stuff would go. It came out gray, not white. Inside and outside the house the same thing, inside and outside. They used to do it every fall.

🔥 The log cabin had two rooms and four windows and real flooring. That was unusual. I don't want you to get the idea that I feel abused, but it is so noticeable if you do anything financially or materially better than somebody else does, that they don't like it. If you buy a better horse or something, they don't like it at all. Neither my husband nor I cared what other people had. If someone had something far better than we had, we didn't belittle it. As far as we could, we had what we liked. We couldn't by any means have much, though, because my husband wasn't financially progressive.

🔥 The house on the farm was a little log cabin, covered with wood board. It was never warm. I was always fighting the weather, always. We were always going to build, but always the farm needed something. It's got the biggest mouth, a farm has. You need implements, and you need beasties, so that always came first. Thirty years we lived in it.

"When it rained it poured in, and when it sunshined you dried your blankets." As time went on, living circumstances improved. People built sturdier houses when better technology and materials became available. Although in rural areas the extra money earned each year usually went

back into the farm, linoleum and curtains and shelves were gradually added, increasing women's feeling of being at home and offering men the chance to show each other the visible signs of their growing prosperity. A linoleum floor seems like a miracle after a rough board floor!

In the small towns and cities, housing was usually a bit less primitive—though not always, as May Potter told me.

In 1917 we lived at the little town of Tilley, a ghost town. The people who had come in when this land was first opened up had built little shack houses. There was a big hotel there, and one little store still there. We had a little shack to live in. Somebody brought a bed spring with a wooden frame. I looked at it with misgivings and said, "Just lay that out on the grass; don't take it into the house." I examined it and found that each of the little pegs from which the rope was stretched was full of skeletons of bed bugs. I didn't know what to do about them, but I had to get rid of them. I did have some candles, so I lit them, one after the other, and burned every little hole, burning all the little skeletons and all the eggs. By the time I got that all done I had to wash the bed springs because they were quite black with smoke. Then I brought it into the house and we went on living.

Milking the cow, Elk Valley.

I found a large box in which they had shipped young trees to be planted. It was the right size to make a couch, so I put my feather bed and a nice cover over it, and some cushions at the back. I used an old sheet to make curtains for some shelves on the wall. The most trying thing was that there was no drinking water in Tilley. It was brought in in big tanks on the CPR train from Calgary. A cistern had been dug next to the railroad track. They'd open a tap in the car and run the water through a trough into the cistern. Then the people would go haul it out with a bucket. One day I was standing by the window. I saw the train stop, saw the water run down, and saw a man with his team come up, put the bucket down, bring it up, and water his horses out of the bucket. I told my husband, "Now, that's the straw on the camel's back." From then on I had my husband go as soon as the train came in to fill our barrel right as it came out of the trough. That seemed pioneering to the nth degree.

Part of the difficulty for some women lay in the need to adjust to something so different from what they had been used to, and from what they had expected. Physical deprivations reminded them of the distance they had come; when keeping clean and warm were so consuming, the culture and community left behind seemed like another world. It was "pioneering" for sure, and "different from the life I was used to" for someone like Annie Gold, a doctor's wife and herself a trained nurse, who came to Lethbridge from Ontario in 1918.

We found a vacant room over an empty store. There was no heat in our part of the building, and when I think about it now, I don't know how we lived. We bought a kitchen stove and a kitchen cabinet that looked like a highboy; it was the pride of my life because it had deluxe gadgetry. Frank would have to carry me out of bed over to a chair, the floor was so cold. He couldn't do it now, but I didn't weigh as much then. I weighed under ninety when I was married, and I was ill. I had sinus strep infection and tonsil infection, and then the joints in my hands began to increase in size with arthritis. It spoiled my hands, but they were never beautiful. It was hard for me to do some things, like the washing, and even harder to wring it. I often wonder what my clothes must have looked like. The Mormon women were wonderful housekeepers. They had wringers on the tubs, but we were just starting.

The washtub was our bath, too. It was fine for me, but Frank couldn't sit down in it because he was too wide. It was a corrugated tub. We'd put it on the floor in the kitchen by the stove. You'd keep the oven door open and we'd have our bath. To fetch the water Frank had to go down twenty-two steps and half a block around the corner to the pump. Then he'd have to carry it all back out again. I suppose if we hadn't been so much in love we'd have been cold. It was quite different from the life I was used to.

In the coal mining towns, mine-site housing provided to managers and their families by the company seemed "comfortable except for the bed bugs in all the walls and joints." In cities and towns, boarding houses or rooms carved out of stores with "great big shop windows" were the first residences for young married couples. On the other hand, some people from eastern Canada or the United States brought with them beautiful white pine for construction, or finely carved doors, or leaded glass windows and even, for one well-proportioned house I visited near Athabasca, three stained-glass windows from Ohio to set among oak-paneled walls. Not so much of that, though; most people gradually accrued only a bit more comfort, a bit more cleanliness on the farms, or moved closer to town.

We had a nice little house up in the west end of town, and I had always had to walk three quarters of a mile to go anywhere. I had girlfriends in town. They knew everything in the area that was going on, these girls. I told them, "You know, we're going to build a new house and I would like to get down-town because I've had to walk so far all my life. Do you know of any lots?" "Well, yes, there's those lots of Dr. Brown's. But he won't sell them." Well, one Sunday night I said, "Let's take a walk." We got going and my husband said, "Do you think you're going down and ask Dr. Brown about those lots? You might just as well stay home because I know he won't sell them." Nevertheless, I kept on walking, walked right up to Dr. Brown's, and thank goodness he was home. Knocked on the door. I said, "Dr. Brown, we're not sick." "You're not? Well, come on in." "I might as well tell you what it is I want. We're going to build a new house, and I've always had to walk about three-quarters of a mile to church and to town and everything, and I would love to get downtown and live here right alongside you folks." "Well," he said, "I don't know what I've kept those lots for. I'm going to sell them to you for just what I paid for them." So he sold me the two lots and the little cottage that was on the place for seven hundred dollars.

In clothing, as in housing, women attempted to reproduce the style they had once known as appropriate for themselves and their families. Some of them, like Viola Carter's grandmother, insisted on perpetuating distinctions between themselves and other people, seeking signs that they had not entirely succumbed to the wildness of the rural frontier.

❦ Grandma made me a dress, navy blue, of quite a nice serge. She put a strip of velvet, about four inches wide, around the waist and the wrists. Oh, how I hated that dress! Still, I had to wear it to school. I think this kind of put me back. I was always backward and would never get out and do anything the other kids did. I think it was because of the clothes I had on, although when I come to think of it, theirs couldn't have been even as good; but it was in my mind. Boy, if I didn't take that off when I got home, I got what for! Then I'd put on a little cotton dress, or a skirt in made-over material. We wore these long black stockings, high up on the thighs, and even then we weren't very warm. I didn't have far to go, but I don't know how my cousins ever made out, walking three miles.

City people who came with some money were able to continue looking as they had in the east, like Ellen Gray from Ontario.

Driving the horse and buggy, Calgary, 1910-12.

❧ People would dress quite formally for an event. Their clothes were made by seamstresses. We had one who was English. The dressmakers would go to your house; you would speak for them for spring and fall for a week, and they would come every day. I don't remember any ready-made clothes around 1900, except coats. My first one was advertised as a "squirrel-lined, fur-trimmed coat." That was my first grown-up coat.

Most people accommodated to the demands of frontier lives without that kind of help, sewing new clothes, re-making old ones, and yet still concerned with matching aprons and pants that looked store bought.

❧ Mother was a wonderful sewer. She had learned it in her girlhood days. We used to do an awful lot of making over of clothes. We did a bit of ordering by mail. But most of our shopping was done in Calgary because the stores were very much the same as they are now. You bought everything in one place; not a grocery store, but it had everything in it. My youngest brother was very short and stout. Mother used to have a lot of trouble getting clothes for him. For everyday the men all wore coveralls, never blue jeans, but pants under overalls with the bib.

We used to buy lovely cotton print and make our own house dresses. Mother and I always liked an apron the same as the dress, so we used to buy enough to make an apron, too. I well remember the first boughten coat. I have a picture among my snapshots of myself up on the roof shingling my first hen house; that is where the old coat ended up.

My husband, before he was married, used to do commercial steam plowing and threshing. He wouldn't wear anything but what he called engineer; they were the blue and white bib overalls. With that kind of clothing, the buttons are put on with steel shanks, and when they come off they usually take a chunk with them. We had what we called bachelor buttons; they were a metal button with a little shank, with a little separate button on the bottom and a spike that came through. You just shoved that through the cloth and pushed the button on top of it. I sewed for the boys, too; I even made their pants. We had quite a time because you had to put the fly in and make them look like boughten ones or they didn't like them. I was fortunate enough to have an uncle and a cousin in Calgary that were businessmen who were both big men. Beautiful cloth we used to get in men's suits. They'd invariably wear the pants out, but I used to rip apart the coats and make what were called Oliver Twist suits, the kind with the short pants that buttoned on to the upper part all the way around. I did my sewing after I got the children off to bed.

Hair styles were also altered to fit the demands of the environment.

One day my husband had gone to town; this day I was doing the wash. The water had to be taken down from the creek, so he had left me with a big supply. I thought it was enough, but I had to get more later in the day. I was scrubbing away, hot and tired and bad-tempered with the heat. I had always worn my hair in two braids I wound around my head. These blessed braids kept slipping down. I went into the house and got the scissors and cut them right off! That was the first bobbed hair out here!

As women participated in the labor of the farm, doing outdoor work that in other times and places had been considered men's work, they increasingly shed women's clothing styles. "On the farm at Crossfield I was dressed like a man. My uncle bought me a pair of those big overalls they used to wear, and a pair of boots, a smock and a cap." Thus outfitted, rural women did heavy work, "men's work." They provided no evidence that they found their roles in conflict. It was often a "case of existence," as one of them said. Where each family worked on its own, with little transient labor available or affordable, who would clear the acres of brush, or cut into the prairie, or plant the poplars for wind breaks? And in the cities, who worked in the family store? The women would, just like the men, and then go on to tend the stock and look after the chickens. Mowing, pitching hay, stooking, raising pigs, trapping, and fishing: women did them all.

I could plow or disk as good as any of them. Our daughter, she's the same way. To see her you'd think she never turned her hand to do any dirty work; but she's a worker! Her and I, the year she went to university, we picked blackberries enough to buy all her clothes and everything to go to university with. It don't matter how dirty a job it is; if it needs to be done, Rose is there to do it.

I was always out there; I brushed land and planted gardens and had cows and chickens, helped with the haying. Then I had my inside work. There wasn't much time to sit and stare; about that time you felt like going to bed. I least liked doing housework because I was so used to being outside. But I used to do all the baking and cooking whether I liked it or not. When I had my boy, I done the same: took him with me where I went. In the garden I'd make a thing for shade and he'd sit there and play in the box. He never complained. I'd put him in a pen in the barn, and he'd be playing in there while I was milking the cows. He was really good.

❧ My folks had just the ox, in 1911. Mother mowed and raked and pitched hay. I don't think she ever stooked grain. The ladies around here didn't sit inside. I know, because I stooked—I never mounded grain—and I've done every other job, I think. I liked it and so did Mother. Of course, I graduated from horses and went into tractors when they came out. Then there was wood and water to get, and I fed pigs and fed cattle. I pumped water for the cattle, too, because we lived down there where we had to pump water. And cold days—there was no school in the wintertime—Mom would take so long to pump and then it was my turn. Oh, it was bitterly cold sometimes while Dad was getting hay for them. The hay had to be hauled because it was stacked in those days out in the field. And then we'd feed the neighbors' milk cows, too, or any other stock. Shipped the cream to Edmonton; then later the Northern Alberta Dairy Pool moved to Westlock. Mom sold hundreds of pounds of butter to the lumber camps. And eggs too. And bread and I don't know what all.

❧ It's funny; I'm a consumer now! We buy our eggs. I buy my butter. It's quite a change. I used to make around forty pounds of butter a week. We had the poultry too. In wintertime my hen house would hold about a hundred and thirty. I had a great big long yard just to the south of me, all hen yard. I'd have up around two hundred until I'd have to put them in for winter. Then I'd have to get rid of some of the pullets because you can't crowd them. I started it right from the time I was married. First I could have just a few, until we got the larger hen house. My husband built covered nests, with a lid on top; you lifted the lid to get your eggs out. They sat out in the open until it came wintertime, and it kept them really healthy. I like the heavy fowls, though they always claimed that you got more eggs from the laying strain than you did from the heavier birds. We used to dress all our chickens, sell them all dressed. That was quite a chore. It would come in the fall just before the harvest; then you'd have all these chickens to dress.

❧ I was always out with my husband, and we worked. Until we moved to town I was still working in the field and plowing and harrowing. We never hired people to work with us. Even when the children were small I had to go out haying and stooking and everything, helping my husband. The children had to look after themselves in the house; I wonder why they didn't tear the house down. I was always outside and they were inside. But I didn't need any help. I was strong and healthy. Sure, I got tired, but it's got to be done. Especially at threshing time;

the menfolks got their hours and went to sleep and I had to work sometimes all night to get my work done: baking bread, washing clothes, I milked a lot of cows, sometimes fourteen. We churned the milk and sold the butter; sold eggs too. It never seemed lonesome to me; I always had enough to keep on.

One year I raised eight blind pigs. We didn't know for a week after they were born that they were blind. We had them penned in a little place so they couldn't get away from the mother. They didn't have an eyeball or anything, just the holes for the eyes. The whole litter was like that. So every morning, and then every two or three hours, we'd climb over and put them on the tit. We got the eight little pigs on the tits and they drank, and they were beautiful. They got nice and big, and somebody said to me, "How the hell are you going to get them on a truck?" "Don't you worry, I'll get them on."

My husband and I fed them and looked after them. The price we was selling them pigs at was so poorly it was terrible to sell them; all we got was four dollars a piece, two hundred pound pig. The man that used to come and take the pigs and cattle in said, "Well, Mrs. Davis, how are we going to load them up?" "Leave it to me." I went with the bucket calling, "Piggies, piggies, piggies." The shed was quite a way from the chute. I'd put the bucket close, and as they came over I backed up and backed up until we got in the yard and then I backed up the chute and we got them in like nothing. The men couldn't believe it. They put two or three boards across so the other pigs couldn't touch them; they might have eaten them up because they were blind. I was very proud to raise a bunch of blind pigs. The price was terrible, though; it wasn't worth the work.

We all learned trapping from my dad. I used to go with him when I was small, just one day at a time because I couldn't go too far. At that time we used to go any place at all. Now you can't go no place without a license. You can't go near a trapline. It has to be your own. My mother didn't go very much; that's why she doesn't know anything about things like that. It's funny, eh? She was born in the bush but doesn't know anything about trapping. Then I always would go with my husband. I lost my old man three years ago this November. We had cabins on the trapline, about ten miles from McMurray. We used to go out by train, with all the dogs; now they made a road. We carried flour and lard, butter and tea, some jam and syrup. That time you can kill most any kind of meat, rabbits and chickens; not much fish, just the graylings. The children sometimes came with us, holidays, Saturdays and Sundays.

❧ I've done a lot of trapping, right here around the farm. I got foxes and rats and weasels. I skinned them and boarded them and sold the raw pelts. You never slit anything except the beaver; they're made flat. I just watched the rest of them when they were doing them. I'd try most anything. Ride horses. Break colts. Up here my husband, two of his brothers, my father-in-law, the four of them would go way back in the mountains, six weeks at a time. I couldn't go because I had to look after the cows on the place. I'd trap around here, twenty miles on the snow-shoes or skis looking at my traps. One winter I got three fox, fifty-some rats, a wild mink, and I guess a couple of hundred weasels. Lynx is such a nice silky fur. They say they're back again now. I know I've spotted them from the house. All kinds of things: if you wanted to fish you got a willow stick with a hook on it, then come back and take a .22 and hunt partridge and have a big feed of them. No reason for anybody to starve; there was lots of food.

In only a few instances did women tell me that men's and women's work did not overlap. It would be more accurate to say that in some families, the women did not participate in their husbands' work, in very few indeed. Men, by contrast, very rarely did women's work. The coal mining communities were exceptions. There, it appears that women in no way shared their husbands' work place. Nor did they socialize much with their menfolk. Instead, women met with other women during the day, while men met after their shifts in public places like the Canadian Legion hall or the Labor Temple. "Our work was in the home," concluded Kathy Reid when recalling the early days at the Canmore coal mines.

❧ I don't think many of the women knew what the men did in the mines. Their men would come home; they'd see to their food and their comfort. They were hard working women and good homemakers, but that was as far as it went. That was the attitude in those days, that a woman was responsible for the home and the man for the pay. You might hear a casual remark if they came home cranky and miserable; if you asked them what the problem was you might get it that way. But they didn't volunteer any information. Certainly we knew a lot about the mine as a whole, but not through our husbands. The women were acquainted with each other, and the men spoke freely in the wash houses. They talked about politics a lot, of course; and that did affect our lives. Whichever government was in depended whether you got lower or better wages. But it was a subject that the men discussed. Our work was in the home.

Her conclusion about the separation of women's and men's work places was not often repeated by other women. Many more of them indicated instead that they watched the work their husbands did quite carefully and inquired about it often, prepared to help out and sometimes to take it over entirely. In the north, where trapping was often done by the Cree, the Hudson's Bay Company counted on Native women to aid the traders. "The Hudson's Bay usually had some man as factor who was married to an Indian woman or girl, or not married, because it was to their advantage so that they could speak to the Cree or the French," said Judith Ashford of Slave Lake. Doctors' wives often worked with their husbands, as did ministers' or missionaries' wives.

All the doctors in the small towns around Magrath were in general practice; my husband, Frank, was on call twenty-four hours a day, seven days a week. I went with him on calls very often. One night we went to a concert in Raymond, only twelve miles away. Just as we got there, there was a cloudburst; the rain was pouring down. We had to stay overnight but had no nightclothes. I got into Frank's white shirt because sleeping nude was not part of the morals of those days. It would have been indecent for me to go to bed without a nightgown. We were not yet asleep when there was a knock at the door. The doctor in Raymond had got a call that a woman back in Magrath had been struck by lightning. We started back the twelve miles; it had taken us twenty minutes to get there and two hours to get back. The doctor from Raymond was driving, and Frank would have to get out to find where the edge of the road was, because we slithered all over the place. We got through without disaster, and went to see the old lady. She had been sitting by the stove with her dog; the dog was killed and she was charred from the waist down. The train to Lethbridge left at six in the morning. Frank put her on a stretcher and I rode with her in the baggage car. All the while she talked about my health. She thought I was quite fragile. And I knew she would never live because a third of the body was burned. I suppose a visit like that we'd get a dollar. Frank couldn't ask poor people to pay him. He said, "I feel like a parasite when I go to see sick people, when I knew the reason they're sick is because they're poor."

In Ontario when she was young, Mother vowed up and down she'd never marry a minister; she was a flippant, outgoing person as a girl and didn't want to be tied down. Dad was a machinist at the time she married him; it was after that he became a minister-missionary. She then had duties as a minister's wife. On the reserve she went out with him to the sick Indians, brought them home, and doctored them up. She would try to teach the women different ways of doing things in their houses, and how to fix them up.

On farms, women sometimes took over the work entirely, as Barbara Gold did in 1929.

❧ Mr. Maples asked my husband, "Do you think you could come down to my ranch and give me a hand? Could you get away?" We had just feed crops, and a bit of wheat. We talked it over, and I thought I could manage; would try anyway. I ran the farm and we did well that year; nearly two years before he came back again.

I found Maureen Edwards's account of her involvement in her husband's farming particularly poignant. She felt his disappointments so keenly, empathized with his exhaustion so warmly; but the disappointments and weariness were hers too.

❧ We didn't put trees in when we came in 1914 because we didn't own land. My husband was just working out for people. I cooked for the men that summer. Then we went out to run someone else's place. It got very depressing, especially when you'd have a nice crop. You'd think you were getting on to where you could see daylight, and then there'd be a setback, like hail or drought that threw you back a whole year. A whole year. So you had to sew, and make over the things, again. You had the bare necessities; when you made cakes you didn't have nuts and the fancies. And you made your bread and your butter; you bought your sugar and your oatmeal, but otherwise you didn't buy.

When you get started farming you can't just up and quit because you're in debt. You owe for horses and maybe a couple of cows, and you've rented the land from someone else. But my husband loved to farm. It was all just hard work—and luck. We've seen it where there'd be a beautiful crop of wheat this high, just ready to take the binder to it. Then, maybe a hail storm would clean this person out, and the next fellow wouldn't get touched. It would snake around, say, through High River, then maybe cut a swathe cornerways and go right down by Nanton and clean some people out. Other people's wouldn't get touched. And I call that luck. It just takes the heart out of you because you're left with so little.

It was just work, work, work. But he just loved it. I never held it against him, because I'd got in the groove. I decided to get married and come out; my family were against it. I did it on my own so I thought I had nobody to blame but myself. Anyway, you didn't have time to feel sorry for yourself. And the men couldn't help it. They had worked so hard until they were almost broken down. Then, if a woman didn't hold up her end, that made it hard. We all nagged, I suppose, but you couldn't keep it up continuously. And you had to feel sorry for them the way they worked.

Those poor men were in the field from seven in the morning until six at night, out in that sun. Brown until they were the color of that chair. Be it windy or dirty, they stayed there; had to. Break their backs pretty near, but they roughed it through. They'd come in at noon and feed the horses. You'd have a good meal ready and another one at six o'clock. You had to have those meals right on the dot because they had to get going again. If you didn't he couldn't have his fifteen minutes to lie down and rest. That gave him new life. If they missed their sleep it was awfully hard, so you just stayed home and cooked.

It was different in the winter. The winter was hard. Some years were bitterly cold and lots of snow. I mean really hard. They'd haul grain in the winter to the elevator; maybe they couldn't get their grain in. So, it rained hard on you, or the sun would blister you, or it was cold.

Lots of times my husband went to the fields with the horses and it'd be real warm, and maybe the odd time he'd forget his coat. Then I would walk miles to carry that coat, the wind just piercing. You'd never get done if you ran to the house every time you forgot your coat. They worked so hard and they put in so many hours.

And with all the hours, the anxiety, the exhaustion, and the work, some people remained poor despite their labor. For some there was a measure of success: travel, perhaps, or greater comfort, or education for their children. Others prospered, their husbands buying section after section or business after business. Few of them, though, forgot the hard work that did not necessarily bring prosperity.

🌿 Back in 1910 a lot of people coming into the Lethbridge district thought they were going to make it. A family from New York came out then. He was no farmer; he'd been a businessman. They were living in the hotel. The doctor asked my mother to go and see her; her baby had got pneumonia so Mom used to visit with her. They only lasted a very short time. When she went back to New York she was our saving grace for the next ten years. She must have had clothing given to her because a lot of it looked as if somebody had tried to alter it and couldn't, had sewn black thread on a blue velvet dress, this sort of thing. Evening dresses, all kinds of dresses, coats: my mother clothed us with what came from that lady. I don't remember my mother having a boughten coat until 1927. I can remember the excitement of the blanket coat with leather buttons on it. And the doctor's wife used to ... well, my dad wore the doctor's suits until the doctor retired from Brooks in 1939. This was what being poor was all about: the stinking smell of egg sandwiches in a lard pail for school every day.

Comfort often came from the thought that "we were all in the same boat." Of course that was not true; some people clearly did better than others. But it was self-defeating to look at them and yearn for what they had. Women instead compared themselves with people in similar conditions, and felt fortunate that they were not poorer than they were. Knowing that they had little, they tried not to long for more.

We were all the same. There were no big shots, like they say, or poor ones. The mine sometimes didn't work for months, and you made it. You had to. You lived on what you got. If you didn't have anything, you still lived. Once they had a nine-month strike here. They used to have a company store that gave a bit of credit. The company store used to hold us over. The store gave many of the people credit and when the strike was over they'd pay for the credit and the back balance. They were never out of debt. Some of them are not paid yet, but the store just scratched them off. This part of the country wasn't as bad as they were down east. Real down, in New Waterford, Springhill. That's where all the poor people were. I can't say we really suffered. We ate. Even the doctor, though—he was one of those guys that if you got sick in the middle of the night he'd get out of bed and come stay all night. He didn't get any money either. If you didn't get paid, he didn't get paid. But we were all in the same boat. Nobody said, "I've got more than you have," because nobody did have any more.

Oh, this was good compared to down east. I went to the company store down east—I was only a little girl going to ask for the groceries—where they'd go to the office and check your time. If the old man didn't work they'd just come down and say, "I'm sorry, but no time, no groceries," and you'd go home with nothing. Pretty rough, I'm telling you. Here when old Frank was there in the store, this was good compared to down east. He was the Santa Claus; he was one of these soft guys. Never let anybody suffer. He had his family here, was an old-timer, so he knew all the people. And he ran the store for a long time, so I guess it was all right with the company.

Everyone was more or less in the same boat unless someone had inherited land from their parents. They were on a different footing. They were on easy street; but not the ones who started with their bare hands. We never tried to ... we knew what our position was and we never tried to follow the ones who were able to do things like go to Banff for a weekend. We knew we couldn't, so you just accepted it. Sometimes maybe you felt you'd like to be going, but you knew you couldn't so everybody took their own road, hard as it was sometimes, especially when you were younger. But you learn to. And then there's children, and there's school to think of, and a pony for the first boy because he had four miles to go. It's to be hoped that children today never have to go back to that.

Even when there wasn't much money, we still had what we needed. You know, I've seen the time when we had five dollars in the house for months on end because we never spent anything. No place to go, no way to pay anyway ...

Mom and Dad got along very well. They kept track of everything and knew where they were at. They didn't want to run into debt. Some farmers plunged in so deeply, and later had to go into bankruptcy. But Dad was more conservative, and Mother said, "We're not going to run ourselves to the point of losing the roof over our head." Then, after I started teaching, I helped to pay the taxes. But Mother always said that, though years have been bad, we could always do with less.

Poultry class at Olds College, 1920.

So, the effects of poverty were clear. Contrasts abounded and deprivation exacted its price from the spirit of frontier people.

❦ My dad was one of the bosses in the mine, so he did get a bathroom. As
a matter of fact, they took a bedroom out of the house and made it into a bathroom for us when we came in 1916. Very few people had running water in the
mine site houses. The houses were quite cheap, five, maybe nine dollars a house
for a whole month. The light was a flat rate, too, maybe a dollar and a half.
Food wasn't cheap; top prices in the company store, though the company
allowed them to buy on credit. Most of them had great big families. The
women did their own washing; very few of them had washing machines. Had
to alter clothes for the child coming up; this was their job and their life and
their interest. They were busy. I don't think they really wanted anything else. I
don't think those people were reaching—not looking ahead for anything better because to them this was it. I think perhaps they were too busy to worry.
And making a dollar go as far as it would go.

❦ I didn't know I suffered from poor eyesight. All I knew was that I had to
sit up front if I wanted to copy from the board. It finally progressed to the point
where I had headaches, and the teacher told Mother I should have my eyes
tested. It was a matter of months before I got glasses. There was flu in the meantime, and the winter months, and we were forty miles from the city and ten from
the railroad. Then, finances must have had a lot to do with it. I had to wait for
Dad to sell a cow before I could get my glasses.

❦ But this is what made me so mad: twelve dozen eggs we'd bring in to the
store and get $1.44. A penny a piece. And I'd make this butter and work so hard
at it. Oh, it was hard work making butter and having to wash it and wash it and
wash it, and get fifteen cents a pound for it. It wasn't worth making, really.

❦ We could write back home to England only to our good friends when we
came in the '20s, because we never had the money to pay for stamps. A four-cent
stamp was a lot of money to pay. We used to make our bread last for so long and
the margarine last so long. Lots of times we were short, but we never said anything to anybody. If somebody came and we didn't have a cake baked, we'd make
the excuse that we'd been too busy.

It was a terrible hard life. I never thought we'd ever live this long. But when
you've got a good man it makes a difference. Yes, he was a very good man. He'd
do any damn thing. When we lived in Calgary he used to go and knock on

ladies' doors. "Would you like your snow shoveled off the sidewalk?" And she'd say, "How much?" "Give me ten cents. It isn't very far around the house." "You do this very often?" "Oh, whenever I get a chance." Well, then, Mrs. So-and-so might like him to shovel it for her. Or he'd go dig a lady's garden. "Give me a dollar, and I'll dig your garden and put it in for you. Twenty-fourth of May everything should come up good." She'd give him a dollar and he dug it up and put it in. Oh, he done so many jobs for a little bit of money.

In 1916 we came from Roumania. Years, we saved to get a farm. It was what we wanted to do. A half-section first, and then later on the ninety acres beside us at Torrington for nine hundred dollars. But it was all bush and rocks, so we cleared that. Then afterward we bought another farm a little south for seventeen hundred dollars. That was too poor to clear; just for pasture. But it was what I wanted. I worked hard through all my life when I was young; in the old country I had to work in the field already. I was used to work.

There it was, then. One worked because one had to. Survival demanded the labor of women in the urban household and on the farm. Survival was the real trick. Despite all the hard work in the world, one could by no means be sure of success. The unpredictability of weather, of crops, of the price of beef or lumber, and of international trade, all signified to urban and rural frontier women that despite one's efforts, chance played a role in one's fate. Beating fate, mastering the environment, if only a little, might bring quiet pride—but not too much; tempting the gods was dangerous. The best, perhaps, one could derive was the knowledge, to quote Magdalena Weiss, that "I was used to work," and then continue to do it.

Working Out

"Working out," they called it: working for pay. Mostly before marriage, but sometimes afterwards, too, frontier women contributed their labor to the marketplace and were paid for it. They worked to support themselves when they were on their own, to contribute to their parents' households, to add to the family income, or sometimes just because they enjoyed it. The work they did was as varied as the economy and as diverse as the mentality of the period and the place would allow. Despite limitations, women worked out, and in doing so, began to find new places for themselves.

Some jobs or occupations were inaccessible to women. Among these were the best paying professions such as medicine (although a few women managed to be physicians, usually practicing far from cities), or managerial jobs in department stores or banks. Tradition assigned jobs requiring strength to men, even though women had provided their strength for generations in factories and farms. Coal-mining and lumbering were among these. Some of the women who stooked grain or snowshoed along their traplines might have had the strength. Nonetheless, even where labor was short and skilled labor much in demand, some jobs were not "women's work."

As women moved into certain jobs, workplaces lost their male nature. Sometimes the work was devalued and lost status because it was performed by women. Other jobs were created by twentieth century demands, like department store clerking. As women worked for pay, their realms widened. They came to value themselves more and began to prepare the

131

way for the entrance of future generations into more and more workplaces.

Working women learned new skills and met new people. Their confidence in their capacities began to grow, as they made tentative steps beyond unpaid toward paid labor. Most women worked because they had to. They took jobs that were easily accessible, not requiring the specialized training or education that most of them lacked. Because their labor was not highly skilled, it was poorly paid. Their work was also devalued as "women's work." There was a sense that it wasn't right for women to work for pay. "Girls didn't go out to work. They would either be teachers or nurses, and that was it. It would be a terrible thing to go into an office to work with a man," said a woman from Medicine Hat.

On the other hand, listen to another woman who worked at a large number of unskilled jobs. "A few became teachers and some went into nursing. But I didn't have any opportunity for that." And still, even without energy and opportunity, more and more women had to work.

Those who worked for pay usually expected employment to be temporary, until they married, or until they could buy a house or farm. As a result, few of them thought of themselves as workers, and therefore did not pressure employers for higher wages, shorter hours, or better working conditions. Most women who worked, in fact, felt lucky to have a job at all, even in an economy where workers were scarce and markets growing. Organizations of working women lay in the future.

After 1900, women worked at jobs that were by then assigned to women, such as sewing in factories like Great Western Garment in Edmonton, nursing, or teaching. Others worked as domestics—cleaning, cooking, and looking after children. They worked as waitresses, hospital aides, hairdressers, tailors, post office clerks, and bookkeepers. A few became telephone operators or clerks in banks or Western Union employees. Some worked with their husbands in drugstores, greenhouses, or general stores. They ran boarding houses and maternity homes. Cashiers, publicity agents for the Chautauqua, newspaperwomen, trappers, and fur traders—women were all of these. It was a motley list of occupations, as varied as women could make it, all the while learning skills and developing faith in themselves. "How are you going to get enough income to live and not be a burden on your people?" they asked. The search for economic independence would, in time, lead women toward self-reliance.

Even domestic labor provided wages, low though they were, and time to call one's own. "From fifteen on I worked out, in Edmonton, and before that Slave Lake and Wabasca. Just the odd place in with a family. It wasn't like at home. At home was always work from morning until night, and working out wasn't. You were through in the evening; you got days off." Domestic work also taught women new ways of doing things, and a place in which to convey old ways to other women. "I'd say that my mother in Italy does it this way, and we'd exchange a lot of ideas." Work gave new meanings to their lives. "I taught three out of the five years between my graduation and my marriage. The first year of my teaching was, I think, the most useful year of my life. I look back on it with nothing but happiness."

Teaching school, one of the few professions open to women, offered women a new arena. Fitting well with stereotypes of femininity, it gave women an audience in the classroom, allowing them the chance to enter the public realm. The career was often a difficult one, usually beginning with teaching assignments in remote hamlets, distant from the physical comforts and companionship they had known before. Teachers were often lonely and isolated, sometimes afraid. Rural towns professed to welcome them, yet paid them poorly, sometimes not at all. Social standing separated them from women their own age, their education from other townspeople. Schoolrooms were often inhospitable, hostile, barren environments for teachers and students alike. Still, women persevered in creating classroom spaces of their own.

Margaret Jones, witty, curious, and a fine raconteur, devoted her whole life to students, first in small villages and later, after a university degree in science, in Calgary. Now nearly blind, but still living independently in a small house shared by several cats and dogs, she recalled her earliest years in teaching.

I had just finished high school. The only way I could think of to get a school was to answer ads in the paper. I got the largest one room school in Alberta, up at a place called Lillyfield. It was largely Russian—well, there was no English-speaking child in the school at all. There were eighty students, grades one to eight, and one teacher. The next year there were eighty-two. Roughly speaking, I would think that if you tagged off everybody's nationality you'd have found about two or three percent Americans, thirty percent Russians, and another thirty percent of Ukrainians, and then the rest of them were a scattering, mostly Roumanians. It was convenient to know Latin if you had any Roumanians.

They were largely folks who had come from farm lands, and taking it by and large, they were very nice. And quite proper about a lot of things. There was one old lady in the town I wanted to become acquainted with, a woman called Popovitch, and I didn't know yet which Popovitches were in the class. I used to see Mrs. Popovitch sitting at her door and I thought what an admirable woman she was. She was quite stately and very clean, and she was nearly always spinning on a spindle. Some of them had spinning wheels but she had a spindle. I very much wanted to make her acquaintance. So I went to the boy that I knew to be the cleverest and asked him to teach me the proper Russian salutation that would take the place of the English "good day" or "how do you do?" He taught me a phrase that I now know is about as dirty a phrase as you

Teacher with her class, Blindman School District, c. 1905-10.

can find. I knocked at the door; Mrs. Popovitch tells me to come in. I walk in, and there she is spinning at the spindle. I thought I said, "Good day;" in fact, I said, "Castrate me." She just rose like a queen and pointed to the still open door and said, "Good day." Well, I soon found out who her family were and got it all explained and we became friends.

The death rate was quite high; her eldest son died of TB, sort of TB and cancer. He had great big growths and yet he coughed as if he had TB. It was a terrible sorrow for her because her husband was dead and she depended on this son to carry the masculine part. The next son was twelve when his brother died.

My first job there—well, I should say first order: it wasn't a job. A job is sometimes dignified with a little money, but not this. The Department of Education sent to me and said that most of the children in that area had never been registered at birth. So it was up to me to get a pencil and paper and go around from home to home and get the name of the child, the date of its birth, its present age. I would go around and the conversation would be like this:

"Good afternoon. I want to ask you about your children. I have Marika in the school and I have Vasileny in the school. But I think you have some more children."

"Oh yes, we got three more."

"Well, I would like their names."

And they would give me their names, and somehow there were two Vasilenys. So then I'd persuade her to change the child's name. I changed one child's name to Evangeline. If the Department of Education knew about this they'd chop my head off. And then I'd say:

"What's the child's birthday?"

"I don't know."

"Was the child born when the snow was up?"

"No."

"Was it born when the crocuses were blossoming?"

"No, no."

"Was it born when the tiger lilies were blossoming?"

"No."

"Was it born when the potatoes were being dug?"

"Yes, yes."

And then you'd go into the potato digging process and you'd figure that possibly the child had been born in September.

"Was it the first of September?"

"No, no."

And so finally I'd say, "All right. It was the twelfth of September." Arbitrarily, I'd give that child a birthday. You know, when you got over seventy households like that you got a little weary of it. And there are children up there, I'll bet, old men and women now, who have the names and birthdays that I tagged on them.

At first, all I knew was to whip a kid soundly. I got better after two or three years of it; I realized there were other ways of handling things. There was a lot of stealing. The kids couldn't help it; they had no money to buy pencils and scribblers.

Every school around had a Christmas concert, and I thought of all the ways to use it to teach the kids to speak and read and write English, and sing. We chopped down a fir tree and put candles on it. We had a lovely little Christmas concert; everybody was happy. The next year, they were building a second room onto this school, and I got the board to permit me to take some of the wood they had already used and make a stage. The kids wrote the play in English and did Russian dances. Using some rather scarce cash, I had made the kids

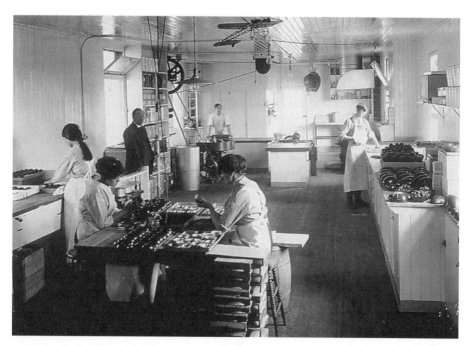

Interior of Hepburn's Bakery, Edmonton, 1916.

costumes; the play was "The Sleeping Beauty." Of course, we had to have seven fairies dancing around her bed, and the little elves. The kids had done excellent work. When the play was over the mothers and children came rushing towards me and flung their arms around me; they were so happy.

Then a guy jumped on stage and said something in Russian. I didn't know any Russian, but I knew that my little girls suddenly all began to cry, and a lot of the women did, too. It turned out that he had jumped on the stage saying that I was a very wicked woman to be running their school. The children had been wearing wings; only God and the angels should wear wings. Well, I had always been under the impression that birds wore wings, too! It wasn't that the people turned against me; it was just that they felt it was wrong to have this person who had done something sacrilegious. They fired me that very night.

In my second school I taught eight children; it was such a change I didn't know what to do, and I was so lonely. I made friends with the old bull they had. He liked me to scratch his forehead and kiss him.

One of the children there wanted to be a nurse. She used to take two or three days off for menstrual periods. I sympathized with her and all that but, gosh, you've got to grit it out. She mispronounced about nine-tenths of the

Postal workers distributing mail, Lethbridge, 1913.

words in the dictionary. I used to correct her; if she wanted to be a nurse, they would doubt she had education if they heard the way she spoke.

I used to do everything I could to keep those poor kids warm. Talk about all the devilish pieces of architecture, the average country school is the worst. The hangers for the kids' clothes were just inside the door where they couldn't possibly melt the snow off. The school stove was back in the school, so that it didn't heat the area. I used to make the kids bring their coats inside and hang them over the back of the desks around the main parts of the school. That way they would get their clothes fairly warm. The children coughed and they had prairie itch; you would come out all spots and itch and itch. And all too often there were pieces of asbestos. If you really want to set a house on fire, put a piece of asbestos up against the wall and heat the asbestos. The asbestos will then heat the wall behind and the house will catch fire nicely. I had a friend whose school was burned that way, and she had to teach school in the chicken house after that.

A little girl came to school limping once. I didn't know what it was, her foot was so dirty. She'd been walking in the mud. She said, "My mama say you fix." I had no way of heating water properly, except on the Waterman-Waterbury stove. The person who invented the Waterman-Waterbury stove should have been subjected to capital punishment. You couldn't boil things on it. I did sometimes manage to get a bit of soup for the children, but it wasn't very often. Anyway, I managed to get a little warm water—one couldn't have said it was pure—washed the girl's foot, and there was a great big boil with pus in it. I said to the girl, "I've got to make it bleed, or it'll get worse." And she took her foot in her hand and twisted it until it bled. There was a great big splinter of wood, about the size of my little finger, on the inside. I fixed her foot up and put her on my horse, took her home, and told her mother how to look after it. Whether the mother knew what I was talking about I don't know. The girl was one of the stupidest I've ever seen. But she sure had the courage to force that wound to bleed.

The people there thought school teachers were nuts, a little bit touched in the head. They didn't welcome me in that town. I was very glad to get away from that school. I once did my shopping with a couple of bachelors, going to the nearest town twenty miles away. My landlady gave me the most outrageous bawling out. My manners, my morals ...! She wanted the two bachelors for her own girls! Actually, I think it's quite clever to have gotten along all these years without being married.

Women who prepared for teaching at university loved the experience. It was hard to leave. "There were moments that you felt quite depressed because university literally became a second home, a second mother. Then you were suddenly torn from it." The years at university led only to one profession, to teaching. Normal school, of course, also provided the training for teachers. Many women taught with far less education, too. Jehanne Casgrain began teaching at a very early age in the school her father established for the village. Originally from Quebec by way of Wisconsin, her English was delicately accented.

I took on my schoolteacher duties at Lac La Biche when I was twelve. My dad was the head of the school in 1910. There were children that needed school here in a new community. They built me a little log school. I didn't go to the mission school in Morinville to study music; I understood that my place was here with the students.

I could help them. I could teach them to read and write, to sing and pray. There wasn't no wages, remember that. That was just on our own. My dad, of course, he was the inspector. I needed somebody like that. One of the boys was my age and was kind of fond of me. One day he stopped studying. I said, "Listen, get to your lessons. Why do you come to school, if you don't want to learn?" He said, "I come to look at the teacher." When my dad came in, the inspector, all the kids stood up. He come in; my dad had blue, blue eyes and there was a little gleam of heaven in them. He said, "I hear there's one of the students that comes to the school just to look at the teacher. That's nice; you can look at the teacher if you wish but you must do your work. If you don't, you'll be expelled." That worked. He didn't want to be expelled. Okay! That was fine!

Mme. Casgrain's experience with her school board, i.e., her father, was obviously a good one. Many women, by contrast, had great difficulty in rural teaching, working with school boards unwilling or perhaps unable to spend much money on their children's education. Often poor and uneducated themselves, they begrudged paying teachers' salaries. I heard stories like Edna Stanton's often.

I had fifty-three students in my class in 1918, north of Lamont. I did a hit and miss job, I must admit. The inspector came out. He said, "What is wrong here? I'm stumbling over children." Three children in a seat, you see, and the aisles were very narrow. "Well," I said, "I can tell you what's wrong. The chairman of the board is an Irish ex-policeman who has no family. He tells the Ukrainian trustees that if they build a new school the taxes are going to go up tremendously and so they vote down the Norwegian who knows there should be another school." He was almost frothing at the mouth when I told him this story. I said, "It's a prosperous district. There are good crops. There's no reason in the world why they can't have a good school here."

I left there at the end of June and they wouldn't pay me. They hadn't paid me for six months. I wrote the trustees a letter and said, "I'm going to give you ten days to pay me or I'm going to put this in the hands of a lawyer." So, instead of going to me, they went to the Department of Education here in Edmonton and told them how hard up they were. The same inspector said, "They'd better pay you." So I got my cheque right away.

The year I was there they were so mean with me. There was an election and the school had to be closed because that was the place they used for a polling booth. They took a day's pay off for that.

Even when the teaching itself was a joy, as it so often was, the physical circumstances of teaching in small towns might be difficult or downright awful. Miriam Short had reason to think so, telling me with a shudder of her early years in Slave Lake, where she still lives.

When I started teaching in Slave Lake I boarded at the old hotel. Rough, oh, it was rough. It was the poorest boarding place in the world, I think. The forestry men boarded there. It was the only place, you see. The foreman ordered for twenty-five pounds of neck off a beef to Edmonton. They'd boil it in a big preserving kettle, the whole chunk. It was so greasy I'd look at it and it'd practically curdle me. For a change we got baloney. It was clean, certainly, but it was rough. The bedroom walls had knots in them. They weren't papered over. The persons in the next room could, if they were inquisitive, peek through.

A career in teaching English and drama, and later in directing and producing, followed Betsy Muir's university training. Before starting her high school teaching career she took a temporary job with the Chautauqua. Large colorful rings sparkling from her bright red, well-manicured nails, low voice richly resonant, flowing aqua caftan, and immaculately elegant hairstyle—all these intensified my sense of wonder at the worlds she had traversed from the small-town Chautauqua circuit to international theater.

🌿 I returned from the university to Calgary in 1924. My mother came out and liked Calgary, so she said to me, "Let's stay here, not go back to Chinook. I'll look for a house and you look for a job." The place I got wasn't open for six weeks, so I went out on Chautauqua for six weeks. I was advance agent and introduced the talent, that sort of thing. Chautauqua played a week in each town; they would bring out a concert, a play, singers, acrobats. The place just swarmed. The farmers came from all over and stayed for the week; it was the one event of the year for them.

Opportunities for women without much schooling were limited to what is considered unskilled labor. Household work, though physically demanding, was deemed appropriate for unskilled women, consonant with their domestic inclinations. The women themselves, as they discussed that sort of work, recognized its difficulties, acknowledged its limitations, and took pride in its execution.

🌿 My parents worried naturally when I came to work at the hotel in Slave Lake, but at that time as long as you had a job and sent a little money home, you had no choice. At that time I remember there were teachers out doing housework. There was no plumbing at the hotel; in the morning if they wanted hot water you'd have to run a jug up to the rooms. The dining room closed

Great Western Garment workroom, Edmonton, 1918.

Chautauqua advance worker dressed for a performance, 1928.

about eight at night, then we just did the dishes and we'd go and read.

Before that job I answered an ad in the paper for housework. I couldn't find the way, stopped this girl and asked her if she could tell me where this address was. And here she was doing the very same. You could see her actually running to get there first. Sure, when I got there the job was gone. Work was so short and that's just the way it was then. Thank God it's not like that for our own children.

❦ The year we came to Calgary, 1920, there was no jobs. Even doctors had no work, no money coming. I went to the Labor Exchange and the lady gave me this address. Well, Elbow Park is quite a way to go and I had to borrow two bits from my landlady to buy the streetcar ticket. A great big fat lady opened the door. She looked at me and blinked and blinked, and I shut my eyes and thought, "Oh, God, what's going to happen?" I said, "How do you do?" She said, "You're not coming to clean house for me?" "I beg your pardon; I am." "You're coming to clean house for me?" "Well," I said, "You might be big and I might be little, but I can do it. Please don't ask me if I think I can do it. I had to borrow two bits to buy my streetcar tickets to get here today. Now I've got to earn enough money to pay that lady that two bits back." And away I went. It was a seven room house; she'd just moved into it and she hadn't been able to clean before she moved in. So I started from the top and I came right down to the bottom. We had dinner and went on with the work.

At six o'clock home came her husband. He looked at me and said, "You? To clean the house?" She said, "You wait until you go upstairs and see." He went upstairs and he looked and he came down and shook my hand and he wouldn't let it go. He said, "How the hell can you do it? Look at my wife; she can't do it."

Then I said, "Well, I'm going home now." "Where have you got to go?" "First Street West and Seventeenth Avenue. Right across from where the big church is." So he said, "Car's ready. I'm going to drive you all the way home." So we got in the car and he drove right to my house where I lived. He held my arm and helped me up the few steps I had to go. And he put a five dollar bill in my purse. That was a lot of money. Two bits an hour; I was there about eight hours, you see, but he give me five dollars and a big box of chocolates. And he said, "Bless your heart, if we called you again would you come back?" I said I sure would. "How can you do it?" he said. And I said, "Mister, we've had to do it so much since we've been here that I'm used to it now."

Nurse carrying water at hospital, Rockyford, 1921.

🌾 I was very lucky my legs were strong, that I didn't have weak legs. When I started to go to work I was twelve. There was a lady across the street. She was an Irishwoman, had about eight kids and got pregnant every year, poor thing. She was very good. I was brought up with a lot of children and I liked children. Just imagine, eight children. There was another lady that had to go to the hospital. She had a little girl about two years old and she wanted me to stay while her husband worked. I wiped her floor, looked after the baby, everything; a whole month until she came home from the hospital. I think she went to the hospital not to have any more children because this doctor, he was a ladies' doctor, and she was one of those women that could easy get around him because she didn't have any more children. With somebody else I stayed two months. I don't know how much they paid at that time, twelve or fifteen dollars a month. She was a Scotch lady. She was the nicest; she says, "Don't harass yourself, just sit down and have a cup of tea."

Running a boarding house, a hotel, or a restaurant was an enterprise open to women, a business that could make money and yet was compatible with ideas of appropriate female roles. Women saw such work as an extension of nurturance. Widows often turned to such work, and so, out of her great fund of energy, did Edith Mackey's grandmother.

🌾 In Ontario, my grandparents had kept a hotel. Grandpa was a sheriff or something like that, but he was not a person who did very much work. He usually managed to get some job that was affluent but not much work. He didn't do a great deal, Grandpa. It was always my grandmother who had to push things ahead in the family. So when they were building the railroad up north in Alberta, the two boys and my grandmother started making meals. The railroad men on the freight train would run their train up on a siding and come up and get meals. She always had the table set and something ready to eat. The tie inspector or any person who would come, Granny reasoned, would want a room and could have meals. Uncle John would help, but he wasn't very well. He didn't hear well. He would peel potatoes or do other things that needed doing. When my mother arrived, she could help, though she was in a very nervous state for a while, after losing my father so suddenly. There was a time when she couldn't cross the street, she was so nervous. So they did all that, in the log cabin. There were two bedrooms downstairs and two upstairs.

The food was shipped in by train. They had no refrigerators. They used dried fruit and quite a bit of bacon and ham, and canned milk. Their potatoes and vegetables they put in a place dug out of the ground. It must have been very difficult. I was stunned, absolutely stunned, when I saw the way Granny worked. Yet she would sing and the young people would come and she would tell stories. She was a great one for animals, too, cows or cats or dogs or anything.

When she died there was a beautiful obituary, a whole column about how she had come there and what she had done, how many people she had fed who had no money. She'd sent to Eaton's and gotten them clothes, too. I didn't know that till after.

Upon coming to Calgary, Margaret Jones's mother and aunts also found that they could earn money in a restaurant as an extension of their domestic experience. She was six years old when the venture began. "I didn't help much, just counted the copper pennies and occasionally scraped the plates when they came in." The restaurant, while it lasted, provided the backdrop for her activities and inspired a lifelong respect for women's creative possibilities.

Married women in England who went out to work were not quite nice. Here, by golly, Mother had to go out to work. At first she felt disgusted and shamed, but it gave the family something to nibble on! She did housework; she'd been a housemaid in England. My aunt Thea was a cook-housekeeper, and my aunt Belinda was just a cook, a very good cook, but she wasn't too bright. She got married soon after we got into Calgary. It was probably the wisest thing to do. She and my aunt Thea started a small restaurant, and my mother joined them. The place is still there, that little white house with a false front. Some class to us!

They served the same things they would have served in England: roast beef, roast leg of lamb, all kinds of boiled dumplings, stewed puddings. I can still see my brother come waddling in, saying, "Dat ole Marsden"—Marsden was our butcher—"he brought Auntie Thea a leg of mutton and it's not carved," which shows how much he knew about meat by the time he was three.

I don't know just why the restaurant collapsed. I have a strong suspicion that the three sisters were too much alike to endure more than two or three years of it.

Cooking for threshing crews, household work, cooking in the small hospital at Canmore and cleaning there, too: Evelyn Ricci, Joanna's sister-in-law, did all these things until her marriage to a coal miner. A few years later, she returned to work, ironing in a local laundry. She told me about her early years of working out.

You know, farmers always have meat and potatoes, a big meal; all the meals are big, because the men started to work out at seven in the morning. I remember that one time I cooked for threshers. I wanted to make money to buy my high school books. We fed about twenty-eight men, two of us; I was fourteen, she was eighteen. Up at four every morning, had to bake all our own bread, a huge batch of bread. We'd mix it at night and then push it down in the morning. It had to be out in the afternoon to the fields. Breakfast for the threshers we'd have porridge, fried potatoes, and four dozen eggs.

Another farm I worked at, the woman had a bad heart, and we had five workmen, so I used to get up in the morning and make the breakfast at five o'clock. They were very nice to me. When they went to town, I went with them on a Sunday or a Saturday night. I was very, very lucky. She was quite young and he was very old, a real good fellow. He'd been a sailor at one time.

I worked back and forth; I'd get tired and go home for a while and rest up and then I'd go back and get another job. I was never out of work, for which I was very fortunate. I never hit a bad place except one time. This lady was teaching. He was a very nice man, but I knew she had a terrible temper and was very hard to get along with. They weren't getting along too well between themselves, you see. This time she came home on the weekend, I guess they had a big fight. I was in my bedroom. I had the door shut but the light was on—I was in bed reading—and she came dashing into my room and picked up my coal oil lamp, and he came to the door and she was going to throw it at him. I jumped out of bed and grabbed it. I said, "I don't give a darn what you do; you're not going to throw my lamp at anybody." She'd set the house on fire; no one could get out of it. There was a narrow, narrow stairwell, and my bedroom was the first one at the head of the stairway. And she turned on me; boy, what she called me! Then she said, "You're fired." "Fired? No way fired! I wouldn't work for a maniac like you, for any money!"

So she wouldn't pay me. I went to him and said, "I want a ticket to Pincher Creek." He gave it to me, and I said, "Just take it out of that twenty dollars she owes me." He didn't say a word. I say, I must have been an awful brat.

I was at home then to look after my younger brother and sister. I saw this ad in the paper, "Cook wanted at the Canmore Hospital." I thought, "Heck, that's one way of getting to Canmore." So I answered the ad. I told them I was eighteen years of age and I'd been cooking for a long time. Well, that last part was no lie. I had been. I came on by train. The conductor: I guess I looked awful young. I think I weighed only 115 pounds. He sat and talked to me and told me about Canmore and what a nice area it was. They nearly died when I got off. They'd hired a cook that was just nothing but a kid, and they wanted to go on a holiday. After a few weeks they decided I could manage quite well, so they went.

There was just one doctor, one nurse, and one cook. You couldn't have more than six or seven patients at one time. Mostly it was maternity patients, and those that got hurt at the mine that weren't too seriously hurt. They had no operating room at the hospital. Serious accidents were always taken to Calgary. I must have managed. I worked there six years.

Factory work, veterans' rehabilitation, nursing, office work: women did them all.

❧ My brother by this time, about 1920, was working at a candy factory. He said, "They want a girl down at the factory there. Run down." I was old enough then; I was fifteen, so I went. They were dipping chocolates there, and I decided I wanted to be a chocolate dipper. "Oh, you can't dip chocolates," my brother says. "It takes experience. They have to serve two years at that. You'd never want to do that." But when I saw them made I decided I wanted to dip chocolates. So I did. I got to be a chocolate dipper. I worked at that for ten years, and it was all done by hand, too. They sold them by the box, beautiful chocolates.

❧ During the war, the University of Toronto put on a three-month course to teach the different crafts. We went there, and then the western girls all came back out west, back to the military hospitals. It was for the soldiers' rehabilitation. I was down at Frank in about '15; all mines there. The Sanatorium had been a summer hotel, which they opened for the returning men. I didn't like it there; I didn't like being hemmed in by mountains. I had nothing to do with the local people; my life was down at the San. Our environment was just the same as what we'd always been used to.

Then I started work up at the mental hospital. I always called that the most satisfactory work I ever did in my life, because I only had the patients when they were starting to clear up; they weren't physically strong enough to do anything and they were given something to do, to learn to concentrate. That was the most satisfactory work—to see people mentally confused clear up and be normal and be able to send them away.

At the end of the first war, to give the returning troops something to do, they learned basketry, and beadwork, and knitting, and carpentry. It was to keep the men occupied. We had very attractive uniforms. They were green with a white collar and cuffs and brown leather belt, and then we wore a big veil like the nurses. After I got married we weren't paid for doing it; I belonged to the Hospital Aide.

❧ My first job was during the war, in 1915, in public health nursing. We'd an awful time at the start of the health department to get people to come and be inoculated for diphtheria. They thought you were pumping poison into their system. We had quite an epidemic of diphtheria one year, and that was what made them come and be inoculated. From then on we had no trouble.

❧ I was looking for a position when I was seventeen. I went to this real estate office in Edmonton, and they wanted me to go to Vermilion. I went there in 1918. There was a hotel and some stores there, and a movie house. I boarded in a hotel which was over a hardware store. The lady served meals to the girls who roomed there, and I had plenty of company. She had a piano and we used to sing around the piano. We had lots of fun.

When stereotypes of prairie frontier women come to mind, the image does not normally include women earning salaries in exchange for their labor in building a society. Quite clearly, however, women did work, and normally for the same reason as men did: they had to. As they worked in increasing numbers, they began to change their view of themselves and the world of paid work. The "male" world, the public world, began to seem less remote. While access to better paid or highly skilled jobs lay far in the future, women in the workplace learned that they might aspire to economic self-sufficiency. Looking after their own economic needs, the early frontier women paved the way for a new definition of women as productive workers, able some day to make choices of their own.

Let me remind you of Margaret Jones who said, "Actually, I think it's quite clever to have gotten along all these years without being married." Not many women made that choice, but increasingly as they worked for pay, women would begin to value their own cleverness.

DEPRIVATION, DISASTER,
and DEATH

"L imitless possibilities on the frontier," boomed journalists. "Come west, come west," called federal and provincial governments, encouraging the migrations they hoped for. Railroad advertisements helped spread the word. They promoted the population of the west by eastern Canadians, Americans, and Europeans. New markets, new sources of wheat and cattle, new mines, and new cities would enhance the national economy and increase the prospects of individual wealth. To lure settlers to an uncertain land, its glories were sometimes exaggerated and its dangers minimized.

The Alberta frontier, to be sure, did not present some of the dangers of other frontiers. The site of the last land rush in North America, the presence of the law was by 1880 no longer questionable, enshrined as it was in the command of the North-West Mounted Police, and later the Royal Canadian Mounted Police. The grossest dangers of lawlessness were precluded by the presence of governments. Transportation was in place by 1910, the railroads having been completed. Settlers were not arriving to a frontier of total disorder. They could anticipate making their new lives within at least the semblance of organized society. The government's presence and a mode of communication suggested the outlines of order; individual dreams and hopes filled in the details of the rosy picture of a better life.

Nevertheless, the settlers' personal lives were fraught with danger. Physical dangers, often the result of the sort of work the men did—mining and construction—were a constant threat. The farming done by women and men could be equally brutal. Accidents were numerous. Weather's inconstancy, the devastating cold, especially, compounded machinery's hazards. Medical dangers abounded, too. There were few physicians; often they were far from rural residents when they needed them. Emergency surgery presented logistical problems for people living far from rail stations, cities, and hospitals. That very isolation also produced intense loneliness as well as depression, violence, and attempted suicides. A vague but pervasive sense of loss could permeate a settler's soul for months, years, or even a lifetime. Rural or urban migrants often felt cut off from patterns that had previously given shape and meaning to their existence. Far from friends, families, and familiar places, women encountered loneliness, sickness, accidents, and death unprotected by the forms and customs of their former lives. The violence and unpredictability of weather, crops, building booms, indeed of the very landscape, took its toll in the form of anxiety, a sense of drift, and of meaninglessness. Despair might become rage; rage turned to resignation. Anger might turn outward as violence or bitterness, inward as depression.

❦ There were years when I would have cheerfully walked out if it had been possible. But we had no money and were twenty-five miles from a railroad. Where was I to go? And I couldn't leave my children. But it did get me down, I'll tell you. I didn't get depressed; I was more angry than anything. But in time, I got resigned. You got used to it. An aunt of mine came out to visit one fall from Calgary. I don't think she had ever been on a farm before. One evening we had a hail storm, a bad one, too. We walked out after it was over; our crop was scattered so it hadn't all been hit. In the morning she asked, "Did you sleep last night?" "Yes," I answered. "Didn't you?" "No, I was thinking about you and your crop hailed out." Well, you got used to it. It was just one more thing.

Accidents, by their very definition unforeseen, were something one never got used to. Yet they were an omnipresent fact of frontier life. People were crushed, dragged, lacerated, frozen, drowned, or burned. Life was dangerous, and help was far away.

❦ When my dad worked in the mine he was burned thoroughly. I remember when the ambulance brought him; it was a horse and a big grey box. I was holding my mom's skirt. They said, "We're taking him to the hospital." My mother had a miscarriage after that, right away. My dad lay on the hospital floor for a week without being touched. They didn't dare because he was burned thoroughly. My mom took him back home after a week. She put olive oil on him and got all his burned clothes off. I said to my mother in Finnish, "Who is that black man?" And my mom said, "That's your dad." I said, "No, I don't want him."

Ever since, my dad used to get hurt in December. November, the last time, my mom says, "Don't you dare go to work during December. You're staying home because you're always hurt that month." The last week in November he was hurt in the Canmore mines; that's what crippled him. They phoned to say they were taking him to the Holy Cross in Calgary. The first train came through and they put him on and they said, "He'll never come out of it." His brains were sticking out. But he did; he came back. His brain clear as anything, but it paralyzed his one side.

Nor were children immune from disaster. Ella Thatcher's brother seemed accident-prone. Her mother was depressed virtually throughout their childhood. To what extent, one wonders, did the one influence the other's vulnerability; or did they both suffer from the unlabeled malaise of a deprived life?

Joey was born with terrible eczema. The doctor tried various things, but eventually what helped him was a Chinese recipe he put together that he had read about in one of his medical books. Then he got asthma. One time later, Betty was supposed to be watching him. We had an old cook stove outside where Mother used to cook in the summer to keep the kitchen cool. The stove had lids in the center. He crawled up and kneeled by the stove, and this lid flipped up and knocked his eye back. You couldn't even see it. We had to run to a neighbor who got on his horse and tore like mad into Millicent to phone the doctor. He came out and Doris, who was only seven, stood and held the flashlight for the doctor. I don't know what he did, but somehow or other he worked that eye back.

Later than that, when Joey was four, he had gone into town with Dad. As you know, he was asthmatic. Dad bought a box of Cracker Jacks with a prize in it, a whistle on a handle. When he got home he blew in and drew in this little celluloid whistle. They tried to feed him bread to push it down, and Dad shook him upside down, but that didn't work. We were in luck; the doctor got there in no time flat. He had to operate right then and there, to put a tube in for him to breathe. Dad had to hold the kid down and Betty threaded the needle and I was holding Mom in the bedroom, who was in hysterics. Then they took him to the hospital, and when we all got there there was my poor dad sitting in the waiting room with blood all over his hands yet from the operation. We could hear the whistle inside Joey as he breathed; it was only a small hospital.

In four days he was out of the hospital. I picked him up; he was so weak. He wanted to get down off my knee and I put him on his feet. He went down just like a soft bag of sugar.

Edith Low was, as she said, "a prisoner" for three years as the result of an accident she had hardly noticed, a small injury that became infected and, without antibiotics, would not heal. She spent three years in a hospital, years that she survived to become a delightful and witty ninety-year-old woman.

I had the misfortune to have this accident when I was seventeen. I was a prisoner for almost three years because in those days, in 1907, they hadn't penicillin. I had got a terrific bang on the hip, but as I was going to my first dance in a long dress, I never told my mother my leg was hurting. Sunday she asked, "Aren't you going to church today?" "No, Ma, I have this pain." But I raced off to school Monday. The station master saw me and asked my mother, "Are you aware Edith's so crippled?" Mother didn't know what he was talking about, but she watched for me that night. Five o'clock; it was getting dark. She saw how crippled I was. She got a doctor to come out next day.

A huge abscess had formed in the joint. Every movement I gave it irritated it more. He said I had to be put under anesthetic, chloroform in those days. When I came out of it, I heard him saying, "I'm afraid of amputation." I woke right up and said, "Did you say amputation? If you do that, Dr. Green, I'll shut my eyes and wish I was dead." He said, "You're dreaming, Edith. It's the chloroform." Mother was more truthful. She said, "Edith, he'll do the best he can for you, and you will have to do the best you can to be a good patient." So that was that. I went into the hospital. They didn't amputate; they operated. Every second day I'd be put under. It wasn't because I screamed; I didn't. They put me under the anesthetic to dress it. It was kept open like this for three years, to drain. By the time I was back on my feet I was on crutches and twenty years old.

I've seen some nasty things happen. My husband got his finger crushed in a chain one day. We were hauling a dead animal out and he got his finger crushed between the door and the chain. Another time my daughter was in a democrat. The horses bolted and knocked her leg up against the cream pan and it just split right open. I put some powder on it, but it was quite a little time because it had to draw together. Always keep a sore dry. Don't put vaseline on it. On the farm you had to be a little bit of everything, especially because you hadn't any money. The doctor was a dollar a mile, and we were twelve miles out. You do learn an awful lot. When your neighbors got trouble they'd come and fetch you. One, her husband died one week; and thirteen days later she was buried herself. Both of pneumonia. That's how bad pneumonia was. Went to one neighbor, the baby was dying. Two o'clock in the morning; would I come up? It was a new baby and it shouldn't have been out of the hospital. It died right on my lap. She had two or three others, so I don't think it bothered her so much.

Sometimes people were looked after by physicians. Some doctors were recalled with deep affection.

Fire in the Edmonton area destroyed the home of these young children and their mother.

❦ That doctor was the best Christian I ever met in my life. Lord only knows how many people he helped out. When people were sick I'd see him go to the store and buy great big orders of groceries, get them all packed in a box, and put it on their doorstep and not even ring the doorbell. And then the money he'd loan out to people, to start them on their house, without charging any interest. The most they paid him was for maternities, ten dollars for a case. About half of those babies that were born were never paid for. He was on a set salary; the union gave him so much per miner.

> On the other hand, there were also examples of medical ineptness and drunkenness, and just downright meanness. Women, when confronted with these, turned to traditional female healers or learned some of the art of healing themselves. Julia Norman of Slave Lake was horrified by one incident of a doctor's negligence.

❦ I'm going to tell you something that will shock you. When I first came here there was an Indian doctor at High Prairie. He was supposed to be looking after the Indians, though he was white himself. There was a white girl here who had gotten pregnant and was having a terrible time to deliver her child. They sent for the doctor to come to Slave Lake from High Prairie. That was after the steel had gone through, so he was able to come on the train, but he didn't get here too fast, you can believe on that. That poor child had been in labor for twenty-four hours. When he came, he didn't bring a single instrument. He went to the forestry and asked the forestry blacksmith to make him a pair of forceps. The blacksmith was so indignant about it. He said, "Just think what he would have done to her with a pair of forceps like that." That was really a black eye for the Indian Department, to have a doctor who comes up here to deliver a child and doesn't bring a thing. And wants to get the forestry blacksmith to help. What do they know about forging medical instruments? She'd been worked over by that doctor. Finally, these two young Indian girls went in there and worked on her, and inside of six hours they had that baby, after all the agony that she'd gone through.

> Often, in pregnancy and childbirth, white women who had access to help from Métis or Indian women availed themselves of it happily. Midwifery was, in time, practiced by many women, both out of necessity and compassion. Some of them brought such skills with them to the frontier, and others learned it in their new environment, often drawing on the various medical skills of Native women to expand their fund of knowledge.

🔥 Once I was pregnant seven months and I started to flow. I had an old Métis woman who came to look after me. Do you know how she saved my child? It seems funny to say, but she had somebody skin a freshly killed muskrat, and she put the whole skin on my belly. I was thinking I would smell muskrat for ten years to come. "Oh, no," she said, "that's going to go away." And I kept my baby. It stopped the bleeding.

Physicians and women often combined their skills, the one bringing their educated expertise and the other their devotion to the survival of people they cared about. Their efforts sometimes came to naught; Evelyn Fuller and a doctor together saved her baby, while in the same week her husband, a minister, baptized her neighbor's dead baby.

🔥 When my baby was about five months old she got the most terrible cold. I was so green about those things. The nurse delivered milk this Saturday morning and I said to her, "I wish you'd take a look at my baby. I can hear her breathing all over the house." The baby was in a basket. She looked at her and said, "Oh, there's congestion there." She said my husband should go to phone a doctor either from Peace River or Berwyn. If you could get a doctor at Berwyn, that was forty miles. If not, you'd have to get one from Peace River, sixty miles. So he went right downtown and phoned Berwyn. The doctor said he couldn't come until Monday. He had to get reinforcements for his horses, because in that forty miles the trail was built up with high tracks that a horse could step off and break a leg. The farmers had made those high tracks freighting their grain. The horses were fatigued, so he'd changed horses and come on. When he got to Waterhole he realized there was no drugstore. He thought there had been one, but the fellow had closed up and gone.

By the time he got there she was taking choking spells and turning black across the nose and upper lip. I'd just pick her up and walk the floor. I didn't know what to do. He said, "Have you got any mustard?" I said, "Oh yes, I've got mustard, but you wouldn't put mustard on a little baby like that." He says, "You put it on the way I tell you and it's going to be all right. Send your husband downtown to get some cheesecloth and some brown paper and some vaseline. He can get those in the general store. Take a teaspoon of mustard and five teaspoons of flour. Mix them up and put them on a piece of cheesecloth. Then put the brown paper over that."

We got the plasters on her right away. She screamed when we put those things on her. He told me to leave them until the skin was good and red, and then to take it off and plaster some vaseline on her chest, and when the skin was normal to put on more, night and day.

He came back on Wednesday. I was so tired by then that I'd kind of forgotten that she'd quit choking, and thought I couldn't see much difference in her. But he said, "She's a lot better. By the weekend she'll be all right." You know, by the weekend she was up and playing. She was a strong baby.

At about the same time as ours got sick, my husband met a man downtown who told him about their baby being so sick. I told my husband to go down and tell Mrs. MacMillan what we did with our baby. The doctor from Peace River had been there, and had told them that the baby wouldn't get better. It died, so I guess the doctor knew what he was talking about.

This same woman lost twin babies. She was raised Anglican, and she thought that if her baby wasn't baptized in infancy it was completely lost. My husband, who was a minister, said she was so distressed. These little ones were only a few weeks old, and she asked him if he'd baptize them. He came home and said, "That's the first time I ever baptized a dead baby. But the poor woman felt better."

Even children participated in one way or another in looking after the sick, sometimes by fetching help. "In the middle of winter we'd cross the meadows, in the middle of the night, when Mother got really sick. The snowdrifts would be three or four feet deep. Then in spring, we waded through the water across to the neighbors' for help." This was Nina Boston's recollection of her mother's long illness while her father was away in the war. Urban people, as much as rural residents, learned from mothers or books or neighbors how to devise remedies, often successfully, for a variety of ailments and diseases.

If they got sick you had to doctor them yourself. I was saying the other night you never hear tell of croup now. I never hear of quinsy anymore. It seems like it's a boil, near as I could think, in the throat. This would take a long time to come to a head and they'd nearly go crazy. They'd poultice it, a hot bread poultice and a linseed poultice, to try to bring it to a head. And I know with croup, I would take a little coal oil and hold their nose and pour it down the children, to make them throw up. You see, they'd just choke to death otherwise and start to turn black. It was a terrible thing, to pour in this coal oil, but they'd throw up and then their throat would be clear.

🌿 If there was any chance of dysentery during the summer months, we always used a gallon jug and we'd put in a cup of rolled oats and a spoonful of ground ginger. That would go through the water and settle. It seemed to satisfy the men's thirst without drinking an excessive amount of it. If you're working out in the field and you're thirsty and hot, you can overdrink of cold water. Particularly where there were men coming and going, and not used to the water. Then, first thing you know, the men would have dysentery. Epsom salts, too: lots of times my brother used to come in and say, "Mother, mix me up a dose of Epsom salts. I've got such-and-such a man can't go to work this morning." But he'd have a dose of Epsom salts and clean him out right properly.

🌿 In the days before antibiotics, we used to make onion poultices for pneumonia. We also used to have poultices of mustard, but we had to learn just how to make them not to burn the skin. For pneumonia, we always found that an onion poultice was the best. We'd cook the onions in oil, and put them in a tea cloth, and put them on the chest.

🌿 Back in 1924 there was the black fever. A lot of people died here in Jasper. Before they would take the coffin to bury it, they had to throw boiling water over it because it was catching, you see.

The influenza epidemic of 1919 was recalled by all who experienced it as an episode of unrelieved horror. A worldwide phenomenon that winter, it affected Alberta deeply, especially influencing the women who stayed on their feet looking after others. In some communities it killed residents regardless of age, in others it affected the young working men most severely, in still others the children were most vulnerable. In the rural areas the toll was economic as well as physical, because so many people were sick that the stock could not be looked after, leaving a double devastation after the spring thaw.

🌿 The priest was nursing twenty-seven Indians in the church the year of the epidemic. It wasn't a good warm building by any means, but it was a warm autumn and that was why he was able to keep them there. He would try to get those who didn't have the flu to help him. They were terrified, though. They didn't want to do anything; they just sat and huddled.

🌿 If I'd had it when I was carrying the child, there was no hope or if I'd got it during my confinement, there was no hope. It was almost like childbed fever the way it killed the mothers that were pregnant. And the trappers—they found them dead in their little cabins. They were still finding some of them two or three years later.

🌿 My brother got pneumonia with the flu. We couldn't get a nurse any place, but a neighbor whose husband was the manager of the Bank of Montreal had a nurse. This nurse would come over and give us whatever was needed. The town policeman would go around and collect custard and soups that people made and take them to where people were so sick they couldn't do anything. The little hospital sent out two of the nurses with the doctor. They'd sleep in the car. The doctor had a chauffeur to drive him. He'd take a sleep when he could. He just went from farm to ranch, wherever he was badly needed. One of the nurses died. Often when there are epidemics they don't seem to attack the medical people, but this one wiped out the nurses especially, I remember.

My mother never got sick. She would get together great parcels of clean rags. The nurse said that was the sensible thing, for the sputum and so forth. I remember it very, very well. That was about the worst epidemic I know or remember.

🌿 The flu epidemic was probably worst in the country points where there wasn't enough medical care. My mother brought me and my sister into the city.

Widow and child at graveside, Coleman, 1924.

We were here until the peak subsided. It was while we were in the city that armistice was declared. I can remember the burning of the Kaiser and the armistice festivities. If you want to call it that. An uncle of mine sold his store in the country and was just coming into Calgary to enlist when peace was declared; somehow I remember that as a part of the flu epidemic. It was just like the plague. It decimated whole sections of the population. I think that people who were working in groups, like in the mines or the lumper camps, were hardest hit. Mother said that in Drumheller they were burying them so fast they didn't have time to take their shoes off.

My aunt lost two of her thirteen in the flu of 1918. The whole town—about two hundred people—and the surrounding districts was down sick with this dreadful flu. The only people on their feet were Mr. Harry Brown, the man in the little hotel (and he told us afterwards that the only way he kept on his feet was because he drank a bottle of whiskey a day) and the school teacher. She was only twenty at the time. She had come from British Columbia and it was her first school. All they could do was go around and give out the supply of aspirin they'd got from the government to keep their temperatures down. Your temperature was up to 104 or 105 degrees.

The teacher just about gave me up. She fell across my bed and started to cry after she had changed my sheets. I was about twelve. Later I asked her, "Why did you cry like that?" "Because you were going to die that night. Your temperature was so high and there was nothing I could do about it. I bathed you and did everything I could. I was so broken up."

My grandmother wasn't as sick as I. Apparently I got it very badly. She had a pan of snow at the door and would bring it in and melt it for water. We had a little pump in the house, a hand pump which you had to prime. You'd pour some water down and then pump like the devil, but she was too weak to pump it. So she'd have to melt the snow and then strain it to use for drinking water. When Mr. Brown would come, or the teacher, they would pump several dishes of water for us. Grandma was always great for her nice linens. Mary, the teacher, said, "Oh, if I could only take an armload of these linens out. If you could see what people have for linen, and the filth, and the dirt ... It's horrible." This broke her up as much as anything.

They were always afraid to walk into a house, because they'd always find somebody dead. Many a time they'd find maybe three people in the house dead. Father and mother and child, maybe. I remember this old Mr. Thompson; they found him dead. This was just one I happen to know personally. It was cold in wintertime, of course, and when they'd find a body in a house there was no one to bury the bodies so Mary and Mr. Brown had to pull the bodies outside and put them in the snowbank.

There wasn't a doctor there within miles. I believe there was a doctor in Vegreville, but then he had two or three thousand people up there, so he couldn't possibly come down to our little community. We just had to cope. Of course, my grandmother was sick and I was sick, but fortunately, we had a warm little house and plenty of fuel that my uncle had hauled and split in the summertime for us. But out on the farms the worst part was the cattle. There was no one to milk the cows, no one to feed the cattle. They died by the dozens. Also, they had just outside toilets in the country, and no water. Now you sometimes wonder how anyone survived at all.

It seemed to me it went on for months, but I guess it didn't. I know it was a dreadful tragedy even when people did get better. By this time it had snowed a lot, several feet of snow. The bodies were all covered up. They had to wait until spring, until a thaw came, before they could get the bodies to bury them.

The presence of death haunted women's memories of their early years. Death from accident, exposure, disaster, epidemic, illness, and childbirth was part of every woman's experience on the rural or urban frontier. The deaths of siblings and of neighbors, parents, and friends were conveyed in eloquent images or simply factual statements. "Mrs. Robertson," said her neighbor Irma Scott, who was a child at the time, "had what they get in childbirth. Every night Mother would look out and see if the light was on in her room. One night: 'She's gone.' The lights were all out in her room."

Perhaps the saddest deaths, their horror unchanged by their frequency, were those of babies and small children. Did fathers grieve deeply over the deaths of their children? Surely, but because women identified so much as mothers, before everything else, it may have affected them more profoundly. In large part, women found their sense of self through relationships, first the most intimate one, the family. At the heart of the family lay the mother-child bond. The death of a baby was therefore the most poignant and the most jarring reminder of the threat of destruction. The fragility and vulnerability of life were suddenly made tangible; raw chance and unpredictable power were exposed. Mothers might struggle ceaselessly to prevent these deaths, but sometimes their combat was insufficient. For the rest of their lives, they were haunted by the memories of dead children.

🔥 Our closest neighbor lost her little boy when he was two; their only child. She worked in the fields with Tom from then on, just as hard if not more so. And looked after the cows. After their little boy was dead, they made work their interest. They just worked and worked. They were very much hurt. You see, Tom had driven to the door—it was wintertime—and let Mrs. Tom out of the sleigh with the groceries and things, and little Billy asked his mother if he could ride with his daddy to the barn. Mr. Tom unhitched three of the traces of the horses and left the fourth one on. He told the horses to get up. The horses felt the tug, and pulled. It threw the sleigh over and the little boy's head hit a stone. They lived for that little boy, and he was taken away from them. Some people thought it affected Mrs. Tom mentally, but we knew it was grief. You never spoke to her but what she mentioned Billy, even when she was in her eighties.

🔥 We had a lovely little girl, the third one, the one that was born after we came here. She was a clever, pretty little girl. She was just about ten and she was counting the days before her birthday. They took her out of school. They said it was diphtheria. She never recovered. She wasn't quite ten, a few days from ten. She was the sweetest natured child. Oh, it was cruel because we were very proud of her. Her father loved her very much. She used to meet him at the door with his slippers. But being a man, of course, he buried it more. For me, it was years; I don't think I was ever the same again. I don't think anybody can really understand what a mother feels. I didn't want to have to lose her. I couldn't understand why the good Lord would take her because I needed her so badly, and yet He must have needed her more. I think I was bitter. I had all kinds of feelings. I couldn't understand why it should happen to me because I wanted her so. Eventually, I met things halfway, but life was never quite the same. It seemed to me that she was the pick, pure blonde and brown eyes and the prettiest of the lot, and He had to take her.

The women whose babies died knew from the evidence in the cemeteries, the many tiny grave sites, that they were not the only ones affected. That knowledge made the event no easier to bear, it simply made the deaths of children clearly a fact of life.

After our last baby was born in 1928 he was very sick. By then the roads were blocked and we couldn't get the doctor. He just had pneumonia and passed away. The same year my baby died there were four others, just the same, of pneumonia. And in the cemetery in one row. One after another.

Funeral customs varied a bit from community to community, or among ethnic groups. Still, no matter how impoverished the family, they put their most noble effort into the burial of a child. Millie Melnyk recalled burial customs in Coaldale. Although the outer forms of burial might vary, the solemnity of the form was experienced universally as a communal event in which people were bound together by a death.

When babies died there were hearses that used to carry the coffin with two black horses. They'd buy a beautiful coffin, a little white brocaded coffin. Each person got a candle to burn. The priest conducted the funeral in the home; there were no churches at first. When they came back from the cemetery they would have drinks and big cabbage rolls and yeast breads. Somebody would stay with the family overnight.

Nellie Scott, of Finnish background, also talked of burial customs, noting especially that despite the poverty of her mining family, her sister's death was commemorated with a funeral that was as elaborate as they could manage.

Stella got the flu. She was vomiting, too. I looked at her and then went back to the kitchen and told Mummy, "Mummy, come. I don't know what's the matter with Stella." A great big foam thing came out of her mouth, and she was gone. She was three years old. But what could you do? There was no undertaker. You just buried your own. Dad got a little coffin over at the store, a little white one. They put the casket in the front room. I opened it up and lay in it. Mother asked what I was doing in it. "I'm just trying it out." Gee, it was a pretty thing, all lined in white satin.

Margaret Jones, out on her first teaching assignment, felt that sometimes a parent's ignorance contributed to a child's death. Hear the poignancy of the mother's giving her child "only the best coffee."

When I saw this baby lying in the woman's arms, I didn't know if it was a corpse, but I thought it looked the way a corpse should look. And it did. It died within a few days. You couldn't tell the mother that you don't feed babies on coffee. It's funny; you would think that women being built as they are, when they'd had a baby and had milk come into their breasts, that it would strike them that as the calf used the cow's udders, they ought to use their breasts. She was giving it only pure coffee—the best coffee, she said. The nurses at the convent had told her that she must not give that child coffee. I had told her that she was killing the child. The hay rack carrying the little coffin passed the school two or three days later.

Whatever the causes, the deaths of infants and children had long lasting and devastating effects on the whole family. Sadie Parks told me that after the death of two of her sisters, one from the flu and the other from drowning, her father never smiled again. Viola Carter's story was similar.

Aunt Meg worked in the government for about fifteen years before she got married. She was quite young when she came from the States, and was kind of late in getting married. She had three sons. One of them got appendicitis and it ruptured before they could get him to the hospital. He was only fifteen when he died. She always blamed her husband for not getting him to the hospital in time. She went a little mental. We know she did because she acted strange. She would have nothing to do with her husband. It must have been ten years or so until she was all right.

Outright despair or temporary depression were aspects of frontier women's lives that do not fit the myths of "sturdy pioneer stock," a stereotypic description of frontier people that makes them sound a bit like cross-bred bulls. They weren't; the realities of the frontier exacted a high emotional price in loneliness and grief. Personal events, like the death of a child or even a prolonged illness, rippled through their minds and their hearts.

In 1915, when I was six, I was very ill. I couldn't talk, I couldn't walk, I couldn't swallow properly. The doctor didn't want to put me in hospital because he figured the loneliness would be the last straw. So Mom had to nurse me. By the time she got me through she had a nervous breakdown. They worried so much about me, and it was summer, too, when she had the hard work with the garden. It was just being absolutely tired and worried sick. I think by this time the wear and tear of the years was hitting her. I don't remember her ever quitting working, but she cried a lot for years after.

165

The staff at the mental hospital at Ponoka had a label for some of its patients, Betty Pearl said; she had worked there the summer she was seventeen. "There were several 'prairie women' there; they had nervous breakdowns because of the loneliness and the hardship." Most of them, of course, carried on. "Well, you just had to keep going." Just keeping going was an adaptation. Homesteaders and town folk plodded on. Often, they shut down emotionally in order to "keep going." Their range of feelings narrowed when events became intolerable. The limits they imposed on their emotions allowed them to survive the rigors of climate, the inconstancy of men, the loss of children, the absence of family, the isolation from neighbors, the poverty, and the work. "Well, we were all in the same boat," they often said. Or, "Well, I guess we didn't know any better."

✿ I can't remember one woman that had a nervous breakdown. I think possibly they made up their minds that they had to make the best of it. Perhaps they made a special effort for their families' sake. I never remember Mother crying. If she did, she did it quietly and by herself somewhere.

Yet the anxieties were there, and the loneliness. "Sure, you couldn't help but be lonely. You had to keep real busy so you couldn't dwell on anything. Otherwise, soon you'd be crazy." Isolation and loneliness contrasted with a sometimes idealized memory of the life and the land left behind.

✿ I missed Norway very much at first. I didn't let anybody see I was crying about it, but I cried many times. I thought that if I could pack my things I'd go right back, because it was so far between neighbors. There was a house three miles away that way; I could see the top of another house, three miles the other way. That was terrible, I thought, because where I came from we were all living so close together.

The knowledge that there was no going back was sometimes best illustrated by small details, the little reminders to a mother that life was now different.

✿ Many times when I arrived from Germany I wanted to go back. I had my little girls back there, and there I had two little beds for them and everything just nice. I came to Canada and there was no little bathtub for the new baby, no little bed. I found an old washtub, one of those old-fashioned ones. And there I bathed the baby. I cried into the water.

The presence, or the fear, of violence also affected women. Especially when they had to face the threats alone, the nightmares and the dark corners of the mind became vivid and real.

When my aunt came out, in 1892, she had a great fear of Indians. Her husband had to be away to shop. One day she looked out the door of the sod shack and saw a rider. You could see for miles, for the prairie was open and clear. She was terrified. She was sure it was an Indian. When the man finally got there he knocked on her door. She opened it; it was a policeman. She was so delighted. She had so many frights, it was really pitiful.

Another time a wagonload of people came in the evening. She had just bathed her little girls and put them to bed. The people—they were Russians—went into the room and looked at the little girls, turning down the covers. She thought maybe they were going to kidnap her little girls. But they just looked at them and laughed and covered them up again. Then they went out to the well that they used as an ice house. My uncle had put ropes down there and he had meat on one, milk on another, cream on another, and butter on another. Then she thought they were going to be robbed. But they just examined everything and put them all back, laughing and talking their own language. They got in their wagon and went away. It shows how people can be frightened for nothing sometimes. Still, they had left behind so many things they appreciated, and found so much that was strange.

My own mother often had to be alone two weeks at a time when my father had to go for groceries at Athabasca Landing. She had some pretty frightening experiences. One day, she was thinking that my father would be home soon so she'd do some baking. She baked what they called sweetcakes, though they were more like baking powder biscuits with sugar. My father liked those very much. She had heaped them on a plate on the table and was going back and forth to the oven. A man opened the door and walked in. It was the end of October; his feet were bare and he wore a long ragged overcoat and a tattered hat. A tall, thin person he was. He picked up a plate of cakes, sat down in a chair, laid a big knife in front of his feet, and began eating the cakes. My mother tried to ignore him completely. She kept on with her work, bringing those biscuits from the oven.

My brother and I were just little tots. We ran into a room off the kitchen and peeked through the crack in the door. We realized there was something queer, even small as we were. Mother got an inspiration. She went to the back door and opened it and called, "Jack," in a big loud voice. I think she called about three times. We had sense enough to keep quiet. He jumped up and grabbed his knife, went to the table, picked up a lot more of these cakes, stuck them in his pockets, and ran down the lane.

We never knew, but Mother was so terrified that night. She locked doors and put knives in them to be sure they wouldn't open. She told me afterwards that she had the axe at the head of the bed.

At one point during her very difficult first year of teaching, Margaret Jones found that it was simply too much for her.

❦ It was seeing the children at the school that bothered me. One boy used to run around the school yard trying to hit the little kids. Finally he went home, put his brother's hand on the chopping block, and chopped part of it off. As far as I know, his family took no steps at all. They may have whipped him; they were great folks to spank kids. There was another boy who used to run around with a chunk of wood—we were in a forest region so we always had plenty of wood—and chase other kids, trying to hit them on the head. I have never been an athletic sort of person. I had one heck of a time catching him. Normal School hadn't quite prepared us for these things.

One day I was walking along the road from the school where I was teaching. There was a bit of newspaper on the ground and I picked it up to read it. As I turned it over I saw on it a scientific diagram of the interior of a cell. It was something familiar, from another world than the one I was in, and I just stood on that road and blubbered.

On one occasion I got out beside a haystack and was feeling rotten. I picked up my gun and thought, "Well, there's no use trying to carry on." I put the muzzle of the gun into my mouth, but fortunately the muzzle cut the top of my mouth and I thought, "Well, you great big coward," and took it out.

Despite it all, women did indeed "keep going." For some, the loneliness continues to this day. "I am bereft of loved ones now. I have no contemporaries. There's nobody I can say to, 'Do you remember when?'" The lonely island of old age can be visited by the rest of us in conversation, establishing links with each other and with our own past. We can share in women's survival, their despair, and their strength. "I come here 1925. See place: me cry, me cry. Stay home most of time. Awful; sad and lonely and scary. But later, see my cows, my land, my fields. A little happier."

COMMUNICATIONS
and
CONNECTIONS

V ivid representations of loneliness emerge from images of physical isolation, from images of a self far, far from others. The rural frontier provides our fantasies with such images. The red handkerchief waving to offer reassurance that the mind and the senses do not deceive, the hope that neighbors will welcome, the yearning to *have* neighbors are glimpses that provide a contrast to the comfort and the profound meaning of life in society. The isolation of life on the rural frontier and the urge to build bridges of community and love are reminders to us all, wherever we may live, that we derive our meaning not only from a sense of self, but just as much from a context in which to place and understand that self.

The people who migrated to the Alberta frontier left behind many of the connections that provided that context. Language, families, modes of dress, styles of food, and patterns of social relationships—they parted from all of these to set out alone to a land barren of the familiar props. New patterns would need to be devised, some an adaptation of the cultural baggage the migrants brought and shared, others quite new, an outgrowth of the new environment. For some people, the new shapes of social life would prove deeply satisfying. For others, the new setting would seem emotionally thin, so meager that the scope of their inner life would be reduced until a mere shrug of the shoulders expressed the whole range of emotions. For them, the nightmares of aloneness would be a reality of waking life.

Many women relished the chances they had on rural and urban frontiers to shake free of old patterns. They knew they could find the resources inside themselves to build something new; the reality of the new land allowed them to do so. Much of what they attempted to build were the webs of social communication. Few of them desired a life of solitude. The context of the family was insufficient for most of them. Most women valiantly struggled to reintroduce an emphasis on human relationships in an environment dedicated to individualism and personal or familial aggrandizement. The benefits of a new economy for the family and for the individual did not satisfy the urge for social relationships; prospects of reward and profit were not enough. Most women had learned to think of themselves as social beings, and began to create places that would offer the comfort and the meaning of society.

The difficult journeys to their new homes demonstrated well the distance from their earlier homes and lives. The hostile environment, even more than the physical distances, contributed to a sense of desolation. Alberta was a land of extreme, often devastating, climatic contrasts. As cold as anywhere can be, as windy as anywhere can be, a north of endless winter nights; to the people who must protect themselves against it the land was a harsh, alien stranger.

February can be the most brutal month of the year here. If a wind starts up on Slave Lake it's worse than any blizzard on the prairie. If it whites out, you don't know where you are. The best thing is to stay right where you are, if you can stand it, lie down and let the snow cover you until it stops. Wait until you can see a horizon. You have no idea where is north, east, south, or west. And then there's that open river you could walk into. It's open all the time, though it may have a skiff of ice and snow over it; then it's very deceiving. It won't carry a dog. Inexperienced dogs have tried to cross over that thin ice and snow, and sunk right in.

We didn't get around by dog, though; my husband had a team of horses and a lovely cuddle of lynx paw robes. When the trappers would skin a lynx they wouldn't bother with those big feet. The little children would skin them and after they were dry they'd sew them together and bring them to the fur trader. When there were a lot, there'd be enough to make a robe. We had one huge one to put over you, and one small one over the seat to sit on. With a little heater under your feet and the lynx paw robes you couldn't get cold.

Traveling was difficult at best. Roads were sometimes impassable, and in dead of winter, downright dangerous. Still, for all its hazards, travel was itself a lifeline, the road a delicate thread of connections between people and places, between life and death.

❦ Back in the twenties, we didn't even have a team. All we had was a dog team to travel with. We had the homestead off to the south by the little lake, off the highway. I don't know if you've ever seen a carry-all on a toboggan. Well, they can lace it up. My husband put the blankets over me and the baby, and I bundled in. He was standing a little behind, where they stand to drive. "Do you want me to lace you in?" he says. "No, I don't think so." We started out, got to the top of this big hill where there was a lot of spruce, and up at the top was a man from town with a team of horses, loading firewood on his cart. He had a small dog with him, and when the team saw this other dog they started to run. I was never so glad I wasn't laced in. I don't know how I got out of that toboggan, but I just put my arms around that baby and somehow we rolled right out. By the time the dogs stopped, the toboggan had run right under those horses' feet.

❦ For grocery shopping we'd go to Athabasca. Two, two and a half days. You should see the ruts we were going through. Sometimes the horses couldn't hardly make it, and you'd have to stop and cut a road around. So we would carry supplies for several days, for sure, a big load of stuff, blankets, food enough for four days. You started traveling in the morning and by ten o'clock my dad had to stop and feed the horses, and then dinner time, and again about three he stopped again for his horses to eat.

❦ One forty-mile trip took place in the middle of the night, at thirty below. We had a brand spanking new car. Frank had a call in the middle of the night that this man was dying; it was a good man, too good to die. The men said he was going absolutely crazy with pain, rolling on the floor. So I got up with Frank and went with him. Our car had just been delivered from Calgary that day. We left with blankets in the car because I usually stayed in it and wrapped myself up while Frank was in the house. This had been a long trip, and bitter cold, so I went into the house with him. He got the man settled down and comfortable, and then they gave us food and coffee. Then we started off for home. It was just beginning to dawn. The sky was beginning to lighten when the car stopped, out of gas. We saw a farm house, so we got out of the car, putting blankets around it because there was no anti-freeze then. We went across the fields to this farm house; there wasn't a soul there. Even the gasoline drums were empty, so we had to turn and go in the other direction until we saw a house again, across plowed fields covered with snow. I can remember how I felt, so cold and so numb. Frank was ahead making a path; I'd follow him and stumble. I thought I'd like to lie here and die, with no effort at all. But we got to the ranch at last where they fed us, and I went to sleep. Frank and the rancher went out to the car. The car was frozen and the cylinder head was cracked. Our first brand new car! It was a heartbreak, but we felt that we were young and there was nothing permanent about bad luck. The car wasn't even paid for, of course.

Despite its dangers, people in rural areas needed to travel to seek out the physical necessities of life. They reached out just as much for the accoutrements that would grace their lives. Barbara West went to Calgary for orthodontia, while Eleanor Lenham went there for lunch, shopping, and music. The trips went beyond mere travel. They provided socializing and adventures that were fondly recalled.

When we lived out in the country I traveled back and forth to Calgary from Oyen all the time. I had to get braces on my teeth, and came in every so often. I was very young then; here it was the day before Christmas, and I started from Calgary to go home. The train got stuck about twenty miles out of Drumheller, and the snow plows wouldn't work. Here I was in my berth; there was just the parlor car and the sleeping car. It was filled with men. The porter put me to bed, covered me all up with warm blankets, and then we hit this snowdrift. We couldn't go any farther, and here it was Christmas Eve. When I woke up it was Christmas morning, and we were still stuck in the snowdrift. I started to cry, and the porter came along and said, "Little girl, you come and have your breakfast." Everybody was trying to cheer me up because all I could think of was my parents and my brothers opening their presents, with me stuck in the snow. Well, I went back to my berth and looked at some picture books and things that I had. When it came just about lunch time, the porter came along again. He had a box. He said, "Little girl, here's a present for you." I opened it, and there was a nice doll. He had walked into Drumheller and brought that doll back to me.

We used to go into Calgary very often. Before I was married, my family had a seven-passenger car; in the old days people went in for large cars. You seldom went without filling the car; you wouldn't think of driving to Calgary without asking your friends to go. We used to go up frequently. The Palliser Hotel was new then, and we'd go and have lunch, and do shopping, spend a day maybe, or the night. During the Grand Opera season, we went up for a whole week and stayed at the Palliser and went to all the performances. Grandfather was very fond of music, and Mother wanted me to go.

The trips to town were both an event in themselves and the route to a social life. The urge for society overcame most women's reluctance to travel. "That twelve miles by horse could be very lonely," recalled Bernice White of her trips into Olds. Yet she went and enjoyed them, leisurely doing her errands.

In '26, we got the car. I had three people to deliver butter to, and cream at the creamery, and all my orders to put in for the things I needed. We went together by car, for I never learned to drive. My husband would say, early in the afternoon, "Are you ready to go home?" I'd always say, "Listen, I just got to town." See, when I was on my own I just took my time. I drove a team to Olds to do all the trading, long as the weather was half-way decent. When it got too cold, my husband would do it. I'd try to arrange it so I didn't have to come to Olds oftener than two weeks because it was a long trip, and they were working horses, not carrying horses.

I'd put in all the orders, and then go and have a little bit of lunch when I could afford it—often I could—then go pick up the orders gradually and bring everything home. Especially with the horses it was fun coming to town, depending on the weather, of course. I didn't come if it poured rain, though sometimes you'd get caught, maybe in a hailstorm. I usually tried to come on Saturdays, when there'd be a lot of other people in town. You know, that twelve miles could be very lonely, driving the horse. It's a lonely trip. Nothing but sky, and looking across the fields.

Being isolated left some people fearful and timid. The difficulty of getting somewhere was not easily forgotten. At eighty, Pat Atmore still responds with anxiety to the thought of a trip, even within the city where she now lives. "Traveling around," she said, "is still sort of terrifying to we older people. I like my own little area. You just learn one little route and you stick to it." She was not, I think, expressing conservatism or an inability to change, for she had made many changes in her lifetime. Rather, she was shielding the old, often re-opened wound caused by the hazards of getting into town.

Other forms of communication slowly became available in rural areas, which, in time, came to feel more like cities as the number of connections people could make with the world beyond their immediate horizon increased. Film and radio brought the world closer and began to alter the frontier experience.

The first I can remember of radio was when I was coming six and we moved from Millicent to Duchess. That night, we stayed at a neighbor's; 1923, I guess it was, and they had the kind that you had to use headphones, and crack and bang and the noise was atrocious! Later, I can remember the Maloneys inviting us there one evening especially to hear this radio, and my dad going home quite put off because he had got nothing out of it but so much static. We got a gramophone first; I don't remember anything more about radios until after 1926, when we got our first one. First, it was a little table model, and then the ear phones. The next thing you went into was the cabinet, and it was a piece of furniture.

The first radio we had at home, my brother made with a little old tube. It was quite a thing. Time after time, we'd sit around that. We didn't have enough earphones to go around, and everybody would sit around the crock with the earphone in it to listen to the hockey game. First my brother had a little peanut

Women's basketball team, Lacombe, 1907-08.

tube. He put it in a pitcher and he could hear sound! He was so excited that he got sound through it. Then they got him an earphone attachment. Then, boy, when they got them big speakers, those horns, we really had something! And when talkies came in, that was really something. You almost didn't believe it. Every time there was a movie we went, because it was a real phenomenon, those shows in the small towns with portable projectors.

Perhaps most remarkable of all was the telephone, which came to Alberta for domestic use in 1907. It was mysterious and it was expensive, yet most people incorporated it into their lives not as a luxury but as an essential link to the community. The telephone saved lives, conveyed information, and overcame isolation. Meg Eaton's family always had a telephone. "Some people had them taken out. They figured they couldn't afford them. We couldn't either, but we done without other things. We squeezed something else rather than give up the phone because I was always afraid of sickness. When you were out isolated, you always had the phone, which was wonderful."

Women endured frontier isolation, sometimes even enjoyed it, because they realized that they would—must—in time create closeness with others. Kinship with other people could be counted on to mitigate the difficulties of urban and rural frontier life. In creating social life, women who had learned early to define themselves within networks of human relationships set about making a new life for themselves and the people around them.

Social life began for young people in the schools where they first interacted with other children. As they grew older, they began to seek each other out for companionship, aided sometimes by a church group.

Social life was pretty tame by present-day standards. We used to go for hikes up the river and take our own wieners and beans, boys and girls together, or sometimes just girls. We'd sing, not necessarily with an instrument, or somebody might bring a wind-up gramophone. The church seemed to be the base. In connection with the church was also a young people's meeting nearly every Sunday night. They'd have speakers and we'd have discussions afterwards on religious subjects. We went on debating forays throughout the city, upholding one side or another of some discussion—should the immigration doors be opened more widely in Canada, things like that. I think the church more than anything else showed me other worlds. We'd get missionaries telling us about

Woman doing laundry and listening to CFCN's first daytime broadcast, Calgary, 1922.

missionarizing the people, but also they were telling us about the people and what they were like. They taught us that there was something out there that was profoundly different.

❦   The people I was staying with when I went to school in Calgary were Pentecostal people and they didn't believe in dancing. They thought I was very awful because I wanted to dance; I even wanted to go to shows and skate to music. They didn't believe in that. It was quite a wrench to me because I had been used to these things. I was rather unhappy, and finally Mother and Dad found me another place to stay.

Some social activities for young people were organized for ritualistic purposes; those events were less fun than the spontaneous events. "At the convent school in Calgary, Reverend Mother had a feast once a year. Reverend Mother's Feast. The girls were entertained one day, and the boys the next. We all treated it as kind of a joke." Young working people devised entertainments for themselves that seemed to defy what their parents thought appropriate for girls. As economic independence became more feasible for unmarried women in the 1920s, their personal possibilities for independence increased, too. Rather than accepting traditional views of demure female dependence, many of them gloried in the adventures they devised.

❦   When I was working in the bank in Vermilion, I lived in the hotel along with two other girls from the Royal Bank. One young man who sometimes boarded there was an advance man for a show, a Scottish family of entertainers. He used to sing a lot, and we'd get around the piano. He used to sing, "I'm shy, Mary Ellen, I'm shy," which was quite a song! Mostly I mixed with the girls that were living in the hotel. Going out for rides with them was part of my entertainment, which I enjoyed very much. The older girl had the use of the drugstore man's car. I don't know whether she ever had driving lessons. She would talk to herself all the time, telling herself what she had to do. She had a Scottish accent; if she'd see a clump of bushes that she couldn't see beyond, and there might be a car coming, she'd say, "Blow the horn before the bushes! Blow the horn before the bushes!"

❦   The Roaring Twenties was when I was in high school. It was the day of the coon coat and the hip flask and the Charleston, and all those things you read about. My social life here was actually much gayer than when I went to New York afterward. Certain places were out of bounds to me, like the Plaza, which I thought was a real swinging nightclub, under the Grand Theater. They had a great orchestra there, and what they called Plaza Punch. It was just grape juice with some fruit, but the boys would take theirs and pour the liquor in it. A terrific amount of drinking went on when I was in high school.

I'm sure that all our mothers knew about it, but they never admitted it. I remember a big wedding in Mount Royal, one of the drunkenest in Calgary. The next day a friend phoned my mother and said, "Wasn't it a gorgeous wedding, not like a lot of them. There was no liquor there." Well, we were just roaring, holding our heads. People were rolling down the terrace in their evening gowns. It was hilarious; we had such a ball. My mother knew, even though she didn't admit it, because she laughed to us later. I had friends that would have to go in to kiss their mother good night, and I would wonder, "How did you get away with it?" Because I don't think my parents were quite that naive.

Before we were married, all going around, we'd go out to the Country Club for dances, after a dinner party up in the Sun Room in the Palliser. They couldn't serve liquor there, so everyone would take a bottle in the back of the car. We would run out, believe it or not, in low-necked sheer dresses, sometimes without a coat on, sit in the back seat of the car, have a drink, and run back in and dance. One year I ended up with the worst pneumonia from doing this!

It was anything but sedate. People were no more moral than they are today. When I was in high school, girls packed French safes in their purses. This is true, though they won't admit these things. We didn't all do it. I was brought up too strictly—but some of them were brought up just as strictly. One of my best friends did that. I guess I was a scaredy-cat, but she wasn't. This all went on before I went off to New York. This is when we were in our teens.

Unlike the upper-class account given above, most aspects of social life were contained within the setting of the home and family. In some rural areas, visiting was restricted to relatives, especially as adult women were constrained by the demands of their work.

In the evenings, people would come to our place. Somebody would go down in the cellar and get some turnips. Everybody would get one. They'd cut them in half and take a teaspoon and scrape the inside, sitting around, talking, playing cards, and scraping the turnips to eat. About eleven o'clock we'd go to the double boiler on top of the stove and get us all a bowl of wheat to eat. You'd clean the whole wheat real good and just boil it on the wood stove till it popped.

At my house we had sugar, but we had no cows so I didn't have any milk. At Vera's they didn't have any sugar, but they had milk. They went away to Arizona, came back years later, just about the time of the Second World War. They had a whole truckload of fancy furniture; everything was really nice. We were sitting around one day having doughnuts and coffee. She used to make the best raised doughnuts you ever tasted. "Gee, Vera," I said, "remember the good old days when you used to come to our place and we'd have wheat with sugar on it, and over at your place we'd have it with milk?" She said, "I don't remember." I knew right then, boy, she'd outgrown me a long ways. You never forget things like that.

When we were younger we had our family and we weren't used to anything different. We lived on the homestead quite a way from the others so we had to make our own entertainment. We used to go sliding or skiing out in the bush. We didn't know what was going on outside. Then after I got married, I didn't have time to think of anything else. I was so busy from six o'clock in the morning until maybe midnight. You wash for five people, and then you cook three meals a day besides baking bread for a bunch like that, and churning. I guess the only time was on the weekends. My sister-in-law lived about three miles from where we lived. On Sundays we'd get together, pretty near always at our place. Like I said, we didn't know anything different.

Another inhibition on social life was ethnicity—not so much the fact of varied backgrounds, perhaps, as the barrier of language. Communities whose members came largely from one country, like members of Norwegian settlements who arrived together, had more abundant social lives than communities in which the women felt embarrassed by their inability to speak freely and easily. "I made friends not so easy; mostly saw Germany people because of language," said Magda Ziegler. Then she continued, "The English-speaking people weren't much for company, you know. It was all more themselves. Yes, I was lonely. I'm still."

Other women attempted to reproduce the kind of middle-class social life they had known in other places, seeking intimacy with women who understood the forms with which they felt comfortable. The "at homes" of eastern Canada or England, the calling cards, and the chapters of the

Four women, Crowsnest Pass area, 1930.

International Order of Daughters of the Empire (IODE) were transplanted customs, generations old, with which women who didn't work for pay were comfortable. They served these women well. At the very least, they could value themselves for perpetuating a social standard.

🖊 Mother was in IODE but didn't do much during the war. She was an older woman and was quite willing to be just at home. Her only other interest was the church, although her only real interest was in the home. You couldn't say we socialized much. You had your own friends who were about the same type as you were. I myself visited friends in different cities; I visited a school friend of mine in New York several times before the war. During the war, people went to parties a lot, teas to raise money for the war. It was all pretty much the same people; your friends were your friends.

🖊 Father was a bit of a snob intellectually. He wasn't very fond of visiting. He said, after visiting the farmers in the neighborhood, "I tried to keep the conversation on farming. I might learn something from them. I don't want to hear their views on politics." Mother was very sociable, though. She would visit with some of the neighbors. They weren't a total loss by any means. One family that were also Anglicans were very musical; they both sang. Mother and Mrs. Haley would visit back and forth. Neither of them had a buggy, but they went on a stone-boat. Mother sat on a little box fastened on it, sitting with a baby on her lap and another child beside her, and I or one of the older children would drive the horse. I don't think Mother ever drove the horse herself. Mrs. Haley would come the same way. They had very nice manners.

🖊 Mother had a day, an at-home, once a month. That must have been something we brought from the east. I don't remember much, but I remember the cards, and the pretty embroidered table cloths and tea cloths and little linen napkins. That must have stuck in my mind as something rather special. Mother did a lot of embroidery, and I really think it was a terrible thing to spend hours and hours embroidering. It would have been more valuable to be reading. When we moved to Calgary, I think her home was her principal concern.

Two girls were married from our house; it was because these girls were working there. One girl had been with us a long time and was marrying a fellow in town. It was just tea and cake and decorations: a big pink cake and probably crepe paper decorations. Before they were married they used to go to box lunches, where everybody took a box lunch and they were auctioned off. I can remember these boxes being made at home, fancy boxes. The person who bought your box lunch would be the one you had to picnic with. Some of the girls would tell their beaux which box was theirs, though they weren't supposed to do that.

Social life for frontier women could be as formal as IODE meetings or as casual as a lunch offered to people passing through to claim their own homestead. Both provided a richness of social interaction that women valued.

People were coming into this north country by 1912. My parents enjoyed having land-seekers drop in for lunch or stay overnight. We had a lot of company. Father would see somebody with horses coming on the trail. He'd go to talk to them, and bring them in. He was always interested to hear somebody and tell them where the land was left and so on. One day, after we'd been in the house a year or two, Mother became really annoyed. Father had got some logs to put on the upstairs, and he'd got some lumber. There was some time left before seeding to work on the house. He was going to take the dirt roof off, and the sods and the poles. It was a windy spring day when he got started. Suddenly a team came along the road, and Father brought them in for dinner. There were my sister and I, trying to get a dinner ready and cover everything with this dust coming down. It was Buckley and Carter from the Rio Grande. They came in for dinner; of all the dismal-looking places, a cold dusty day and the dust seeping down! That's the only time Mother felt annoyed; otherwise she enjoyed these people.

The interactions between women, the time they spent over cups of coffee, quickly expanded to become visits among families. Women talked to me about their female friends in one breath, and in the next reminisced about whole families joining together for an evening of music, dancing, and conversation.

Everything was new for Mother to learn. Mom always had a soft spot for Granny Smith because she came over when they first got set up; just stayed and stayed. Not say much, but just chatter: talk and talk. When my parents arrived here, there were four other married couples. There was more visiting done in the early days than there ever is now. They'd pack up on a Saturday night. Perhaps the cow would go along, too, and stay overnight.

❦   There were two neighbors real close, French Canadians. They had a big family, about twelve, I guess. They were the same age as mine; they were always playing together. And I was friends with the wife. There was another woman that was our friend, too, much older than I, but she was coming to see me almost every day. Every day she was coming, every day saying to everyone, "She's like my daughter." We used to go here and there together. A lot of visiting, and in wintertime especially. The neighbors gathered Saturdays or Sunday evenings. Some friends know how to play accordion, violin, clarinet. They could dance and have games in the wintertime, not summer; summer is too short here, you see. Too busy in summer, but in the winter, oh yes.

While most women valued friendship, indeed needed it, a few women, for a variety of reasons, avoided it. Anna White simply said, "I was never much of a mixer. The neighbors were quite close, but we didn't visit back and forth. I didn't have much to do with the farm women around." There was Jesse Baker, who felt alienated for cultural and personal reasons.

❦   I came out as a bride in 1917, and I had all new clothes, nice clothes. I was slow to make acquaintances, so they just thought that I didn't want to. I didn't know this until years afterward when somebody told me. They were more or less in a rut, and most of them didn't have any—let's say—education. And then, I was altogether different looking. I had protruding teeth, two big teeth in front, which were hard for me to keep covered. Of course, there weren't regular dentists then. My teeth kept getting worse and worse until finally I had to have them out. People didn't know me after; it made such a difference. It was a relief not to have to try and keep your mouth covered: I could smile then. It was hard for me; and I won't say they were envious of my good clothes, but maybe they weren't used to them.

Still other women simply hadn't the time to visit. "Never took a day off for anything. We was always so damned busy that we never had time to take off a day, but if we had done, where would we have gone?" Betty Boyd, a black immigrant who arrived with her family from Oklahoma in 1909 and who still lives on the family homestead, claimed the same. "In the evenings I didn't do anything but the same as I did all day. If you wasn't doing it, you was thinking about doing it. I don't think I had much of a life of leisure. I don't really know what that is." Yet others, like Eva Lubchik from Ukraine, isolated by language and distance from the town, quite sim-

ply could not get anywhere. "Saturday, no dances. Nothing. Clearing for the garden with an axe. Never for coffee; no time. No roads across the brush. No transportation, no babysitter, no money. No go."

These women, however, were exceptions in their lack of any social life. Far more typical were the dozens of women who recalled what became a virtual institution—the Saturday night dance. Whether in a home or in a hotel, whether whole families gathered or just the young people, the Saturday night dance, with music usually provided by men, and its sandwiches and coffee brought invariably by women, took shape all over the prairie. The dance was supplemented with other community events such as turkey suppers or Christmas parties or Sunday afternoon visits, as ritualized as the dances. Women began to give form to their urge for community.

The town of Ranfurly was about two hundred people. Down in the little hotel, which was also the dining room, they had a dance; clear out the room, maybe once a month. A couple of musicians would come to play. They had an old honky-tonk piano and anybody that knew how to play would just get up and play. That was about the only socializing there was, except maybe once a year some type of entertainment would come from Edmonton, put on a show. It'd be mostly all young people at the dances. I don't think the older people did much socializing at all. Life was so rough that by this time they were just ready to sit down and rest. I can never remember any of the older people being there. I can remember some of the younger generation, though, about thirty-five, bringing their babies. They'd put a blanket on the long benches all around the hall, put the babies there to sleep while they danced, and sort them out at the end of the evening.

I don't remember many parties in homes. I only remember one place that had parties, at the Thompsons. Mr. Thompson, he had TB, and of course my grandmother had me scared to death. I wouldn't go into their house. They had a lot of parties, but people would never eat anything at their house. Poor Mrs. Thompson; this must have been a heartbreak. She'd prepare sandwiches and have a great big pot of food and nobody would touch anything. That must have been awful.

We had turkey suppers in the fall and they were always a nice thing to go to. I should say chicken supper first, because people didn't have turkeys then.

Everybody raised chickens. You dressed them and you stuffed them and cooked them and you made pie. And what they called the Ladies Aide would get together. The closer people in town would do the arranging. They'd tell each one what they were going to bring. They'd meet at a big hall, and people would come from miles around. Miles and miles. The old ladies were really good cooks. We had these every year. Then most of the boys were taken to war. When someone came back they'd have a nice homecoming for them, a big, big do in the hall, a really special do. They'd welcome these boys, really welcome them.

We had all Germans and visited quite a bit there in Torrington. Usually we'd go to church seven miles, and then in the afternoon visit somebody. German church but English school. Always families; as long as the children were small we took them along, but if they were grown up they didn't want to go any more. Not many dances; just a couple. I never went. When I got married I quit. It shouldn't be, a woman when she raises a family, dancing.

People were more sociable back then, 1907, when I first came to Olds, than they are now, especially the farmers because you'd go to church and they'd ask you in for dinner. A whole crowd of you; and have just a cold dinner maybe. But whatever they had, they invited you, and of course you invited back. Sometimes you were prepared, sometimes you robbed the hen roost.

The school arrived here in 1915. I remember because when it opened up they had a dance at Christmas. Mother and I went over for it. I didn't dance because

Group of women at tea with the minister on Sarcee Reserve, 1890s.

I didn't know how to; to be truthful, Mother was against dancing. She got that from the young girls she had gone with in England; she went to the Methodist. And Father, he didn't like me to go. My uncle Tom was the one that took me to the first dance when I was nineteen years old. He was up here working for the forestry. Mother's youngest brother. "It's about time she's out seeing things." I felt funny, but all the boys they—well, I guess they were happy to see me because I was out there on the farm alone. The only girl on the farm. It's kind of a lonely life when you think it back.

In the beginning in Slave Lake you could count the white women on the fingers of one hand, and then you'd probably have some fingers left over. There were some very nice white women at Kinuso; they were in the same boat. We'd go there for the First of July sports and I got to know a lot of them. We'd sit and visit instead of watching the sports. Some women liked the sports, but I was never very enthusiastic about ball, especially if somebody was there to visit with. After the highway was finished in '29, we'd go often.

New Year's of 1900, the main event was the ball at the barracks. It was given by the officers and noncommissioned officers. All events were formal things in those days, not casual dress. During the winter they had a Quadrille Club. Of course that year I was only twelve, in 1900. I first went to the ball in 1907. In the spring my mother had my coming-out dance at the house. That was your formal introduction. I've got things tucked away here, in my box. Everything was written up in the newspapers in those days. Here it is: "Miss Anne Ives was attended

Italian Ladies' Society members, Crowsnest Pass, 1929.

with the most brilliant eclat which has ever distinguished a home function in Calgary. The great house was ablaze with lights and prominent guests who had come to do honor to Miss Ives, one of Alberta's own daughters." It sounds so silly now. They wrote about pearls; the white pearls were a mistake. It was pearl-embroidered slippers that my aunt had worn at my mother's wedding; my mother's people were from Montreal. After that, I could go to dances, but only with a chaperone. If my mother and father weren't going a lady friend, an older person, would take two or three girls. And all programmed dances.

When I was younger I recall New Year's Day. It was the gentlemen's day to call on the ladies. My mother always served port and sherry wine. The little table would be set with all the glasses and the fruitcake and shortbread. Two or three of them would go together. I used to be quite excited because I would open the door. Mother and the dressmaker made me a little black dress and white organdy apron, which I was very proud of; I used to wear this to open the door.

The ladies all had their afternoons at home. We all had calling cards. I got my silver calling card case after we were married. My husband gave me that the Christmas we were married. Tiffany's in New York. According to some of the books, just a few people did that, but that's not true, a lot of them did.

As institutions took root they, too, sponsored social events. The few young women who went to the University of Alberta supported each other in a largely male environment. The female students were offered the same curriculum as the men, but their social life connected with Pembina Hall, the female residence, was quite separate.

At the university we all belonged to our Waneeta Society. There were no sororities allowed at that time, but this started way back; I know it was going during the First War. We took our theme from the Indians; we had our Big Chief, who was president, and during initiation we all wore blankets and sat on the floor. Favors were little feathers or something else that carried the Indian theme. Our motto, still inscribed over one of the side doors in Pembina Hall, was Indian for "One for all and all for one."

We had what we called our Colonial Ball each year. No men were allowed in, and those girls who could dressed in colonial style as men with long colored bloomers and high socks. We used to turn the suit coat inside-out with the bright lining showing to make the colonial coat. It was a dance; no dinner, though we had refreshments afterwards. We had more fun than a pet pig because we had no boys to be bothered with, and the girls danced with girls. The last couple of years I was there, about 1920, the boys used to gather at the windows and try to watch in. We could have a real good time without them, but it seemed they couldn't without us!

Teacherages became the focus of some young women's social lives; for others the Labor Temples or the YMCA offered a place where men and women could meet, grow, and learn. Life was becoming more complex, denser and richer.

After I got married I was kind of lonesome to get back to teaching kids that I'd taught for so long. I used to think, "The bell's going to ring; I should get busy and go to school." Well, married life was a different life altogether; there had been such a group of teachers together, and the social life's far different on a farm. Isolated.

When we got here to Lethbridge in the twenties, the union bought a hall and they called it the Labor Temple. They began to have plays, concerts, and lessons for those who wanted to write and read in Ukrainian. They had dances every Saturday, and plays and concerts on Sunday. I began going with my sister, and then my mother and my aunt started to go to the Labor Temple.

We had the YMCA here quite early, before 1929, which contributed a good deal to the social life of Canmore. The Canmore Coal Company paid for the YMCA man's wages. Up to that time, there would just be the odd social in the union hall; the YMCA heightened the activities. We had an English paper, a gym—just about everything. After it started there was something on practically every night; debating societies and a choral group and an art group. It became a very busy, very busy town.

Organizations had begun to take over women's attempts to create links in their communities. When women arrived on the Alberta frontier, they found it very strange indeed, for it was a place devoid of social connections. The distances they had traveled underscored their isolation from all that was familiar. They felt alone, like isolated points in space. They needed to fill that space with meaningful ties to other people. Just being there was not enough. Just farming or working or cooking or raising a family were not enough. Thus women began to provide for wider social relationships.

Men came to the frontier for adventure or in order to work, and found their justification in their labor—the fencing, harvesting, the running of stores and providing services and speculating in land. Women did those things, too, and yet they sought more. They began to enhance the meaning of their labor by placing it in a framework of human connections, in a setting wider than the farm or the house. They connected beyond homes, beyond families, toward a community.

The forms of communication becoming available on the frontier helped them do that. The slender threads of roads and telephone wire brought them closer to other women, while the radio, for all its crackling static, and the newspapers and films brought the world to their households. They happily used all these as ways of drawing closer to other people. The most immediate kinds of closeness were the most gratifying. The picnics, the afternoon coffees, the Saturday night dances, and the "at home" afternoons were all forms of social life that women devised and worked hard at perpetuating. At the very least, they benefited from the supportive presence of others; at best, lifelong friendships were formed.

To this day, the remote hamlets of Alberta continue to be united as communities by the congenial efforts of their women. I shared in an evening of laughter and talk at the community center in a village in the north. It is a town populated now mostly by older people. The younger ones have gone to the cities. The women invited me to join them in reminiscing about the "old days." I felt honored to be included in their conversation. They shared not only talk, but true to tradition they each brought a plate of sandwiches, even though we had all had dinner, and cakes and coffee. We would all rise early, yet we lingered until after midnight; and I felt part of a continuum and a tradition—a community.

Towards Community

Frontier women from all backgrounds began to engage themselves in making communities. As neighbors and friends, women's activism in a land without institutions brought a knowledge of their ties to each other and the hope for a future that could embrace them all. In response to the anxiety of formlessness, they created bonds to each other, the bonds of community. The conflict of the migrations they had all made, their arrival in new circumstances, and their interactions with strangers prompted them to seek connections with their new human and geographic environments. They started in small but significant ways, most often in neighborly acts.

When you were in a place like that you had to learn how to do these things. My heart used to ache after the war for the English brides that came out and didn't know anything about a farm. They thought they were getting 160 acres of land; it sounded like a million. When somebody used to condemn them, I'd say, "If someone stuck you over in China and said you'd have to grow rice, you wouldn't know how." I felt so sorry for them.

In our community, when we came in 1906, the women would have quilting bees, not for the church, but just for helping each other. They visited around a bit. There'd be barn raisings, too. Dad gave up three acres of the corner of his homestead for a graveyard because when the children died he felt we needed something like that. There was no church there at the time, so my mother used to invite the people home to our place to have a meal after the funeral.

❧ Other Ukrainians here, not too many; maybe four or five miles away. Sundays, sometimes we visit. If anybody come that was guests. Nobody looked on one another; they were all the same. Worked as hard as they could just so there would be bread to eat. You have to work back for what you get from another person. One place you got your cows bred, so you work for a whole day stooking to pay that back, you see. They were all poor, and didn't anybody do any better because they couldn't afford. They didn't have it themselves.

❧ The town was on the other side of the river, but the stores were on this side. The bridge was the meeting place for the hamlet, you see. Everybody would meet on the bridge. Some were fishing, some were just looking, some were talking, some were catching up on what was going on. Every evening they would gather there. I've seen that bridge from one end to the other just flop, flop, flop with fish the nights they were biting good.

A sense of community began to emerge. As an Irish immigrant said, "All sorts of differences seemed to fade in light of the fact that they were all living in the same community with the same family problems." People brought cultural baggage with them to the frontier; it was retained, altered, or abandoned depending on circumstances and personal preferences. Some religious and ethnic rituals were maintained, mostly on formal occasions; others faded away, sometimes out of the fear of being perceived as different.

Many of the religious rituals that women and their families had observed in other places, in former times, were altered. They had learned elsewhere how to perceive nature, God, the world, and human life in the context of the religions in which they had been raised. Their differences were diluted as the migration, the frontier itself, and the desire for assimilation took precedence over fidelity to the old ways; women sought to become part of a new social environment.

In a few rare instances, whole communities migrated from the old country together. In these, settlers retained old patterns and customs. Coming as a community, they simply recreated the familiar patterns in a new place.

❧ The Norwegian community here was living in great intimacy with one another. It was a cohesive community. They had a simple but strong Christian faith. They were Lutheran people. When my mother and father came in 1895 they spent the night at some bachelor's place. In those places you would be taken in where you came. No doors were ever locked. They got their houses built in the fall, and had their first church service.

They were a singing people. Father organized a choir. They celebrated their first Christmas Eve in one of the family's homes. My father and three others had driven all the way to Edmonton and bought a few small candles to decorate the cake. On Christmas Eve, the choir sang a few songs and then the children recited and sang. Grandpa read the Christmas gospel. They had a little bit of Norwegian baking. One lady brought one kind; my mother brought the butter to spread. Somebody else brought the coffee. And so they celebrated their first Christmas Eve that way.

Some people experienced ethnicity in a negative way: it was something used against them. This was especially true of German settlers who, after 1914 and the beginning of World War One, bore the wrath of their communities. German women felt that their ethnic differences, and later their ethnic guilt, were exaggerated by their difficulty with English. They felt embarrassed at having to wrap their tongues around strange words and, as a result, felt truly like outsiders.

Sometimes it happened that people laughed at me for my accent. One case I never forgot. In a store, yes, and it was the post office, too. The owner had two girls. I talked to one and she stuck herself behind the counter and laughed and laughed, but the postmaster came and helped me out. It's just something that happened.

I felt like a stranger here when I first come after the war, from Germany. They found out that my husband was in the war. The police take my fingerprints. I said, "I am not ashamed that I am a German. Whose fault is it that we are here? It is the government." Once, I went to the store to get some salt and that storeman asked me what I want. I said, "Some salt." "What?" he said. "Salt." He didn't understand. The tongue has to be bended. I cried. When I came out from the store a lady asked me, "Do you speak German?" "Yes," I said. She said, "I speak German and I speak French and different languages. Now I tell you, you have to speak. No use to cry. Go in and speak even if it's all wrong." That helped me a lot. But that was bad. Sometimes I said, "I just can't take it." The people laugh and call the police and everything. And we come from a country where everybody liked each other in the many villages.

The mayor came out one day. He knew we ship cream to the creamery. He said, "You tell me if you want something. I'll help. Tell me if you have some-body that you want to have over in Canada." He said he would help get people from old country. Some were nice to us; some were not nice.

🔥 I went to a German school in east Calgary until 1914 when the war broke out and they didn't want the Germans any more, so they closed the school. From then on I worked out. I worked in the Alberta Laundry. They laid the German girls off there. They just took the English in. It didn't feel right.

As communities grew in size, they grew in complexity, and in variety. While many ethnic groups remained in pockets of the cities or tucked away in hamlets of their own, like some of the small Norwegian or Québécois villages, and while some people felt fear and hostility around them, the demands of the environment began to overcome separateness. Working together, going to schools and churches together, inhabiting a land strange to all, women began to shed their separate ethnic identities. Certainly they noticed their differences. Even while claiming that "the nationalities were really mixed," some people, the Chinese immigrants especially, seemed different enough to notice and unfortunately to deride. If white settlers soothed their own consciences by insisting on their toler-ance, they certainly observed many actions that were far from tolerant. In any case, most white women's social interactions rarely included the few blacks or Asians who came early to Alberta.

🔥 At Airdrie, the nationalities were really mixed. The only Oriental was the Chinese restaurant. We had no Orientals in the country at all, just the little Chinese restaurant in Airdrie. I can remember Mother getting quite upset about a couple of cowboys from a ranch. They went into the beer parlor and got a little high and cut the pigtail off the Chinaman. Well, of course you know, in those days when a Chinaman had his hair cut it was a very disgrace-ful thing. I can remember Mother saying to those two boys, "I don't care whether you thought that was fun or not; it wasn't fun. He is a Chinese per-son and he's still a person." These two boys felt terrible after they sobered up. Now today, they'd blow that up on television, way beyond reason. They get a little story like that; but presumably it would never happen again.

Mostly it was English and Scottish people around, and a few Danes and a few Swedes, and one Catholic family. We went to the same parties. We all played ball together, the girls as well as the boys. It was all done as a community and really, religion never seemed to enter into our lives excepting on Sunday when we all went to church. Mother and Dad saw to it that we did, too!

❦ I can't say I think it was hard being a Chinese person here. Like, when they opened the community center they said they bought the dishes from the Chinaman that had a little restaurant in town; most of the dishes had belonged to him, they said. I mean, I never had any of them in to visit my home or I never visited theirs, but still I never mistreated them. I always treated them like I would any other tradesman in the store. I never done anything mean like I saw one person do: throw part of some mushy thing over a little divider in the store; he just deliberately threw this cantaloupe over and it landed on the owner. Well, that was meanness in my mind. I was sorry that I was in that party.

I guess mostly the people I went to school with around 1910 were Americans. I do remember that at home, in Utah, we always wore sunbonnets. My sister had worn a sunbonnet to school and I saw a couple of the older girls in the corridor. They were sure having a good time throwing it around; belittling the bonnet really. When I went home and told Mother about it, we never wore bonnets any more. See, we were Mormons and should have horns and all that. Mormons have horns more than any other religion! But we'd just keep our mouths shut and take it, that's all. There wasn't any sense making a fool of yourself just because the others were.

❦ The Finn people, we had a hall made of logs. Everybody went: kids, mothers, babies, everybody. The Finns would put on plays, remember? And dances; that's where I learned to dance and gee, I sure love dancing. But parents didn't care if you don't marry a Finn man. I don't think they cared we marry a Chinaman. Well, maybe they do ... This country you can marry whoever you want. I don't care how poor and how rich; if you feel like it, you can marry.

❦ There were Italians and Scotch people, and Hungarians. I had a very good girlfriend who was Roumanian. Yes, we mixed. We had one Negro couple. A lot of the kids coming to school would call them "nigger" if they saw them. I used to go and visit her. They didn't have any children, and I just loved her. I helped her as much as I could. I thought it was awfully mean of the kids. They tried to mix, but when they found out that they couldn't, well, they didn't. Finally, they moved away.

Definitions of "different," which could become prejudice, sometimes arose from fear. Similarly, the fear of being defined as "the other" also could translate into intolerance. When women spoke about the strangeness of other groups, their talk moved imperceptibly to their own apartness and its pain.

❧ I remember the first time I saw Indians. West of Morinville there was a reserve. This wagon pulled past us. At that time they had long hair. Now it's quite in style, but at that time men didn't have long hair, so I was so frightened. I myself was not so happy in the school. At that time, there was French and there was Irish and Scotch, but mostly French. They didn't receive us, being Irish, too well. They made fun of your speech. They'd call us greenhorns. That sticks a long time, and things like that can hurt a child so terribly. Others of Irish descent, not born Irish, were just as bad, saying bad words. I guess they looked on us as immigrants. Really we weren't immigrants because I think the real immigrants that came over were sponsored by somebody who brought them out to work. But we didn't. We came out on our own. Mother was a very proud person, and I think that hurt her, too.

Fear got all rolled up into one. During the nightmare that was World War One, Kate Home associated all "savagery" indiscriminately.

❧ The first I heard of the war I related the Germans to the Indians. What a thing for a child to do! We lived very close to the big library downtown. When we'd leave the library we'd go through the park. Right down beside the gate, in the shrubbery, there were Indians sitting there on the ground. Well, we'd just begun to read books and were reading a lot about the Indians, so foolishly we pretended to be afraid of them. We'd tear past them as hard as we could and invariably, when we got home, Mother would have a couple of them on the back porch. She'd be giving them tea, because they used to go around from house to house in those days. So, reading these books, I guess I associated Indians with savages. Then the war came. I remember one night I had a nightmare. Then I asked Mother and Dad if the Germans were like Indians, because I'd heard them talking about the atrocities of the Germans. My parents settled that for me. I went back to bed quite satisfied.

Native women like Rebecca Courtereille could also perceive differences as stereotypes. She told me, "A lot of white people eat rabbits, too, and talk real good Cree. But they're just white people." Institutions like the Hudson's Bay Company played their part in fostering racial antipathy, as Julia Norman indignantly told me.

❦ "Half-breed" is an awful term. The French people speak of the Métis. I prefer the words "of Indian origin" or "Indian ancestry." I loathe the word "half-breed." I think that the person who first used it had no breeding himself.

When I married my Indian husband, my dad looked grieved. I was one of the original integrationists! My people had come out here from Europe; they couldn't comprehend the Indians. They could only degrade them. Those people who came out here, traded with and exploited the Indians, in many ways degraded themselves. Still, when my father came to know my husband, he spoke of him as "the man."

The priests up here were quite concerned about the young Indian girls. They were in the convents until they'd reached a certain age. As soon as a girl was out of the convent, the white men wouldn't leave her alone until they had her in an interesting condition. The girls had no defense. The families figured that if a white man paid court to their daughter they were honored. It seemed that the white man could do no wrong. A lot of them felt flattered.

I'll give you an example. The priest at the convent was advised that two girls were gone. Frequently, they'd run away. He phoned the police at Peace River to keep an eye open for the two girls; he phoned east and west, alerting the police. Two fellows had these girls. They were stopped at Peace River. These two men were going into the north to trap furs and were taking the girls along as a convenience. The priest said, "Either marry the girls or bring them back to the convent." They married them and took them into the north. They kept them there for about three years. One of them divorced after they got back here, the other stayed with his wife. My hat is off to that man. She developed TB and he devoted his whole life to her.

For a long time, the prettiest Indian girls were reserved for the Hudson's Bay factor. I am indignant when I think of that.

Ethnic integration in communities continued.

❦ Quite a number from the States when we first came up here. Some of them went back. I suppose they would prove up and get their farm in their name and then sell it and move back to their old home. But about eleven miles away they're decidedly Norwegian. We would have community picnics, and if Valhalla said they were having a community picnic by a little creek, all of us bundled into a wagon. We'd go together with our baskets of food and have a picnic. I remember one in Valhalla; we were on the banks of the little stream. It's just a poor little rivulet now. It just poured with rain, so off we went to the hall. They asked people who could sing to come and sing. And could anyone read a story? Recite a poem? And we had a little impromptu concert.

❧ Spirit River wasn't very big then. There was just a few people and you got acquainted with them through the church. A lot of the farmers there were Ukrainians. Amongst themselves they would more or less maintain the Ukrainian customs, I know because we got invited to their weddings. The food was out of this world. We would always try and sit where there was a plant, because we couldn't do all that drinking! I don't know about the poor plants!

❧ If you could mention any part of the globe, you could probably find somebody from there around Gleichen. Our favorite question when we met anybody new at school was, "Where did you come from?" That was always the first question, because everybody came from someplace else; except for the Indians, nobody was second generation. Some of the earlier settlers were British. There were many from Europe. They came in especially at threshing time in the fall. They were paid to come west and do the harvesting. Father would go into town and stop by the Chinese restaurant; there he'd pick up these men who were sitting around the sidewalk and ask them if they wanted a job. I often woke to hear strange languages downstairs. We had Poles, quite a few French Canadians, some Russians, and Scandinavians.

We had German neighbors quite close. A lot of people had come in with the railroad and had homesteaded shortly after '85. Just after '85, Gleichen was the terminus of the railroad, not Calgary. Gleichen had the roundhouse. When the railway went on, everything moved west to Calgary. Then, around 1912, a terrific influx of Americans occurred; many of them came from the western states, and many of them were Mormons. A lot of those people came up with the idea of making a lot of money. They were going to farm on a big scale, make money, and go back to the States each year for the winter. Many of them farmed here all summer, and if they didn't have cattle to look after, they'd take off in the fall and go down to California, returning in the spring. They didn't become citizens.

The Depression put an end to all this. They didn't go anywhere; and they became Canadian citizens. They became our friends and neighbors. All sorts of differences seemed to fade in light of the fact that they were all living in the same community with the same family problems.

There was also an Indian reserve at Gleichen. The Indians were not always confined there, though; they wandered more or less at will. The attitudes of new immigrants towards them varied. Some of them had a very appreciative attitude, while some were quite critical. At one time, there was a rumor that there was going to be an uprising. An Indian killed a policeman who was going to arrest him for drunkenness. The kids at school wanted a little excitement and they talked about this as though it were going to be a major uprising like the Saskatchewan Rebellion. Of course it wasn't that at all. One of the minor chiefs at that time went in under the tent ropes with a lasso and caught this man around the shoulders. The gun fell from his hands. The Indians themselves took him into custody. Father's attitude was that they were all God's children.

Around Oyen everybody had the homestead idea, something like they'd had the gold rush years before. There was a large migration of Americans, but mostly Scotch and English and some from eastern Canada, and a little French and Dutch. But they all mixed. People became so much one in everything that you hardly noticed the difference in nationality. The different nationalities should not go in as a colony; it's bad for everyone. Some of them never learn to speak anything but their own language. In that way especially women are held down a lot. How can you isolate when most of us, in our history, find that we are a mixture? When we came from the States as small children I remember

Group of women voting at Westcott, 1917.

the folks saying you must be loyal to the country you're going to have for your home. Many people brought even the names of the old towns they came from, trying to hang on to something. It's good to hang on to some things, but you can hang on too long. Our parents taught us that where you earn your living is your home, and this is where your loyalty must be.

🌿 Most of the students at my school in Edmonton were sort of Waspish. But I remember one girl, quite a large girl, in grade eight. She had come in from the country and lived as a maid. She was probably not paid very much at all. She wanted to take grade eight. She was much bigger than the rest of us in every way. She was so robust, with bright pink cheeks and lovely skin, just the picture of health. She blushed easily. We knew she was different. The Ukrainians were often spoken of disparagingly by a lot of people, and were referred to as bohunks. It was funny, though. It didn't seem that anybody at school paid much attention to her, and she sat right at the back because she was so much taller than the rest of us. And yet, on St. Valentine's Day, she got the most valentines of anybody in the whole classroom.

🌿 Some of the older generation never really did accept our ways, never spoke our language very well, but their children became part of the social life in Canmore. At first they didn't speak very good English. But we encouraged them to become part of this country. And at the mine, the men had to speak English if they wanted their miner's certificate; to communicate with the other men they had to speak some kind of English, for working orders and safety regulations. The people in my group socialized right along with them, though the mothers didn't to a great extent.

If ethnicity sometimes divided people, religion served to unite them. Most people went to church. The theology of Protestant sects virtually disappeared on the frontier to become merely church attendance. The few women who thought about God found a sort of pantheism in their daily lives. The much larger majority simply went to church, finding there a forum for socializing. The presence of a church, any church, was all that mattered to the Protestants. They went regularly to church, enjoyed services in a thoroughly secular way, and found there a social center in the midst of busy lives. Children should have "a religious upbringing"; women and children provided the churches with ongoing membership. "My father was a Presbyterian, my mother an Anglican. We used to go to both places.

In the early days here it didn't matter what denomination you were." The doctrinal differences that ministers and congregations had once relished had no place on this frontier. Church attendance had little to do with analysis of the Bible, theological issues, or demands on the conscience. "Sure we go to church, United Church. In Poland, the Orthodox. But here, today Catholic come, tomorrow come a different. Doesn't matter."

Churches were built early in each city and town. When the community could not afford a minister, itinerants from the cities paid weekly or monthly calls. "A minister used to come and have church in the schools once in a while. The different people would go, and the Catholics would go to their own if they had a priest in, or come to ours." The ministers' visits were welcome, and so were the lunches that followed. "You're your own church. It's only that you go there as a group together, you get much more out of it. We're all in some way dependent on each other to live." The Protestant churches allowed frontierspeople both their individuality and their gregariousness.

There was an Anglican church here at Beaverlodge, but no Methodist. The church had quite a good congregation because Anglicans and non-Anglicans attended. Some of the ministers' wives were great helpers in those early churches. I remember one especially. They lived in the church house, a large lumber building with a good upstairs and a nice large living room where you could entertain large numbers of people. She always served tea and coffee and lunch after the church services, and everybody would join in. It was quite a drawing card for the congregation.

We went possibly twice a year to church because it was so far with the buggy, but we used to have the rector from Grande Prairie out to our own home. We would let the neighbors know. We are Anglicans, but everybody came that we knew, Methodists, or Presbyterians, or whatever they were, and loved it. We had coffee and buns afterwards.

Mother loved the church. When we went to Grande Prairie, the Anglican church was a funny little two-by-four church. Mother had great taste. The altar coverings didn't suit her, and I remember her telling the rector she'd make new ones. I think the beauty of this hilltop replaced the church for her. It's the same for me. I go to church happily; I like all the neighbors about me and the worshiping together, but I worship just as well in this window looking at God's beauty. Everything to me is a work of God.

❧   We went to church every Sunday. A lot of the time we walked both ways. We thought nothing of it. With us, that was our social life. You went to church not worrying about anything religious, so long as you had your Bible verses memorized for Sunday school. The next thing you went to church for was to show off. If you had been lucky enough to get a new gingham dress for spring, you froze to death wearing it! The next reason you went was hoping someone else would invite you for dinner, because that's the way they did it. I don't like to hear people of my generation get sanctimonious about how they went to church twice a day. Sure, I went to church twice a day, but there wasn't much else to do. Half the time the battery for the radio was in the car. There was no library around to get books, so you were just jolly glad to get to church on Sunday and see somebody.

Sometimes they had revival meetings; both my parents eventually became members. They almost scared me into it. There were services every day for a whole week, with singing and preaching about the war coming and the world coming to an end. I remember on a package of Jello a picture of a deer in front of a very colorful sunset. To me, this was a picture of the world burning up. The ministers would sing, "Oh, brother, why not tonight?" And the congregation would sing, "Oh, brother, why not tonight?" until some of the poor guys that had no more sin in them than God expects of any of His children would be whooping up there at the front, telling about their sins. This one night, they got me feeling like I was walking right into hell. I was almost ready to stand up, and my sister turned around and looked at me hard and that was all I needed to stay in my seat. That night I couldn't sleep at all.

❧   I used to sit with my grandparents in church often. My grandfather was a great singer; I can still hear him singing those old hymns. "Days of our Fathers," he used to shout! We sat one row behind R.B. Bennett, later prime minister of Canada in the 1930s. Bennett had a habit of sitting with his arm on the back of the pew and looking to see who was there, and speak to everybody. I later found out in the church minutes that he would count the people in the choir. If there were thirty-one people in the choir, he'd give thirty-one dollars that Sunday.

We children also went to the Baptist Sunday School. It was only a block and a half away. It did bother my grandparents a bit, but it was so convenient and Mother didn't mind. It was good for us, I think.

❧   The church had been built by Scottish people at the end of the lake. That was where everybody went. It was the school house during the week, and the missionaries, the young ministers, were allotted the school house for church on Sunday. It was Presbyterian, but pretty well everybody went. My mother said we were raised and baptized Presbyterians, but she said she didn't believe in that sort of thing. She said there's twelve gates to heaven; that must be all the twelve denominations. And she said if you lived a good life you don't even have to go inside of the church to get there. You're your own church. "So," she said, "it's only that you go there as a group together. You get more out of it. We're all in some way or other dependent on each other to live."

Now, my son married a Catholic girl. The children have been sort of raised in the Catholic faith. That has never caused any rift. He was baptized himself in the English church. By the time my youngsters were growing up, they were chumming with kids that all went to the Anglican church. So I thought, "If they're going to the Anglican church, why not baptize them Anglican?" I don't think the name of the church means one thing. I don't believe in religious bias because I don't think there's any one religion in heaven.

Catholicism and Judaism provided more structure and orthodoxy than Protestantism. Catholic traditions and hierarchy were transplanted, and the Church arranged for priests and bishops to circulate through frontier areas. For Catholics, church attendance was as much a religious as a social experience, though the pleasures of church ritual were much cherished.

🔥 We had our first parish priest up here in 1915. The bishop came the first time in 1909, the year after we were here, the first white family in the district. It was in August, and the time of the mosquitoes and flies. All the men went out in their rigs to meet him, and twelve young men on their horses. The younger children stayed at home with the women. Just my aunt went out to meet him, as she saw the rigs coming, to have the bishop's blessing. But she never knew which one was the bishop. He had a mosquito band around his hat; she passed him right by and came to the rig where her husband was. We teased her so much about that. We asked her, "Were you looking for the mitre or the crown?" Things happen like that in the beginning, though.

My mother said, "I can't see the bishop coming to our place with just hay on the floor." Dad said, "We'll unroll the rug and put it in here on the floor." When the bishop came in and walked on this nice Turkish rug he was amazed. "I never expected to see a thing like this."

🔥 There weren't too many Catholics here. The priest used to come down from Edmonton about three times a year. He always stayed at our place. Grandma had, I think, the nicest little house in town. He had a big suitcase. It must have weighed seventy-five, a hundred pounds. I had been brought up almost to venerate the priest. So of course I wouldn't let him touch that bag. I wouldn't be maybe ten years old and I would tote this a good three blocks from the train, and I can remember him laughing and getting a big kick out of it because I insisted on doing it.

We had a tiny church up the hill, about a half-mile out of town. A Catholic family out there had built a little, tiny church on the corner of their property. We used to go up and scrub and clean that place. Grandma had a beautiful garden in the summertime, and I had to place all the flowers. There were two or three French families who'd come in from the country, and the farm family, and Grandma and myself, and with all the kids this filled the church.

We were fortunate if we had Mass three times a year. But you might as well have had; on Sunday morning me and Grandma and anyone else who was there had to get down on their knees and she would say the prayers of Mass, and we'd say the rosary. There are five decades of ten Hail Marys, and then she'd say the second rosary for the souls in purgatory, and then for the sick and the dying and those in pain, and anything you can think of: you name it, we'd say a decade. I'd finally go to sleep!

The rest of the community were Protestants, but I don't ever remember seeing another minister there, and there wasn't any other church, so I don't believe they had a service of any kind. My grandmother was a little bit bigoted. Although I can never remember her holding it against anyone or saying anything against them, still—well, she had had to go underground to hear Mass in Ireland, and was born in 1856, just ten years after the famine, so she had reasons to have this feeling, I guess. I used to go to funerals with her and we weren't allowed to sing the so-called Protestant hymns. But I'd go to a funeral with a friend and I'd sing my heart out. Somebody would say, "You aren't supposed to sing the Protestant hymns," and I'd say, "There's no such thing as a Protestant hymn. It's a hymn to God."

Only one woman spoke to me of an experience that was a religious event all her own. Her sincerity pervaded the tranquility of her small Calgary garden on a warm autumn afternoon as she told the story.

❦ We were brought up Presbyterian until we were on the prairie; then we went to the Anglican church. The people bypassed the religion aspect and accepted the fact that this was a Christian experience, not religious exactly. The minister was just one of the neighbors. If there were any need or trouble he was called on.

Through my husband I became greatly enticed with spiritual things. He was a Christian, and I commenced to admire his attitude. On the trip after we were married he'd get the Bible out every night and I'd have to read it. Do you know, I got to hate that book. I remember he went out one night and I took it and threw it across the room and said, "I hate that thing." It seemed so dry and dead to me. Only when I had this spiritual experience did it become precious. I realized early in my Christian experience that the Old Testament was the history of the world, and poetry, and truth.

My husband had had his experience many years before. I became very ill. He told me that I was just to lie there and when I felt myself going out to say the name of Jesus. I knew I was going; I would go down in such a pit of darkness and I would say, "Jesus!" and I would come out of it. This went on until one morning the doctors came and examined me again and said there was nothing wrong with me. And yet they had told me that there wasn't a chance for me.

After that we both felt a very definite call in our hearts. We decided to go to the Foursquare Church in California. My father said, "How could you possibly be a minister? You couldn't compete with these great learned men who have so many letters after their names. They're so wise and they have so much." I said, "Papa, I don't expect to compete with them. I'm just doing what the Lord wants me to do."

Catholics and Jews numbered few on the frontier. Most settlers were Protestants who, despite early religious background and ethnicity, found themselves attending whatever church was available. Truly, theirs was a secular religion. The social aspect of church attendance bound them together; despite their differences they began to cast their lot together. People began to think of themselves as connected to each other.

❧ It was really rough for one family. He was too lazy to go to work. He was just a laggard, and he had a family of five or six children. The neighbors would always take things to them if they could. He just never wanted anybody to give anything to his family. But his wife appreciated what they could sneak in to her. He was a very domineering man. That was first discovered when we went to school. The older boy came in one morning quite upset. He'd be only fourteen, maybe fifteen years old, same age as my older brother. I was just getting started in school. I remember sitting around this great big table and Dave say-ing to my dad, "Well, I think somebody should go over and see what's going on, because he's awfully upset about his mother. She's expecting a baby." Dad said, "I don't know. You can't walk into a neighbor's house and tell him what he has to do." The next day, when we went to school the son said, "I think my mom's going to die. She is so sick. She needs help." Dad thought this had gone far enough. "I think we should go over." The husband said, "Nothing wrong with my wife. She's not sick; just the boy's nature to worry." So you can't go in. Two nights later, the son came to our door, just hysterical. "My mom's dying." So Dad thought, "To heck with this; we're going in." He said to my mother, "Sally, get your coat on. That woman needs help."

When they went in she was lying on a blanket on the floor pretty near frozen to death. The baby was born, and the mother died. Possibly it was too bad that they hadn't come in quicker. But you feel that you can't break down a neighbor's door to come in. Seven children were left. The older ones stayed to look after the younger ones. There was hardly any food in the house for those kids when Mother went in. She said it was just a crime that there was so little for them to eat. The father took off somewhere and left the kids. He was gone for quite a while, six, seven months before he came back. The third-to-oldest one said to us kids at school, "It might be years, but when I'm old enough, I'm going to beat my old man to a pulp." He was still so bitter at his dad. With the help of neighbors they were able to exist; then some relation came from some-where and brought them to Calgary, and the son at my school went on to be a very bright student.

When I was twelve or thirteen years old, another man, Mr. Mackay, died and left his wife. Mind you, she was quite a goer. She could get out there and drive the horses as well as anybody. She carried on with a bit of help. When she was short of horses or harnesses, my dad would give her horses. And if any-body really was in trouble that way—sickness or loss—the neighbors were awfully good. I remember one of the neighbors breaking his leg right at har-vest time. His crop was all taken off by the farmers who all got together.

People needed each other. I remember just one time my dad getting really angry, in the later years. We were having a party at our house and we needed to get cups. Dad went to Airdrie to get those cups, and they charged him rent for them. It was of all people the doctor, who belonged to the lodge where they'd get the cups, who said, "We can't let you have those cups unless you pay rent for them." So Dad said, "Okay, I'll pay rent for them. But," he said to

Mother, "those cups are going to be paid for twenty times over." Mother said, "Now, Joe, don't do it." But Joe did it. We lived in a coulee, just below an S-shaped hill. The doctor's old Ford couldn't make the two-mile haul up that hill. When he got called up the hill Dad would go haul him up. We were always hauling somebody up the hill, not charging anybody. So, the next time he hauled the doctor up the hill it cost him ten dollars. Mother said, "That isn't right. You're making a sick person suffer for that. Next time he comes up you go out and do it, the same as always." So Dad never did charge him again, but he got the rent back for his cups. He said to the doctor, "You never realized how many times I did this for you for free."

I think there was a very, very strong bond between the people. What one had, the other had; back and forth. I guess it was because we were far enough apart. Your neighbors were two and three and four miles apart, and you really needed them.

Quite clearly, many people, women and men alike, desired the anonymity of the west more than they wanted a sense of community. "We immigrants were not exactly interested in city government when we arrived in 1911. We were more interested in starting to build something for ourselves." Many preferred to "keep to ourselves." Others, though, found ways to become involved with other people, and with the shape of the

Women's Auxiliary (Anglican) members, Calgary, 1911.

future. Some women observed people who seemed to exert qualities of leadership and began to learn from them how to be leaders themselves.

❧ Our father was kind of a leader, interested in new improvements, anything like that. He'd pass it all on to the community. Our mother, too; she was one of these little ladies that's happy and jolly and friendly with everyone. If anyone was ill, she was on the job. They both worked together. During the great flu epidemic they ministered to all the sick in the district and out of the district, wherever they could go where there were sick people. They looked after them all, and never became ill themselves. She was a little bit of a lady with dark hair and a sunny, happy smile, and he was a big fellow. Home was always open to everyone.

❧ It was very democratic up north here, but surely it's true that several people went ahead. Mother right away became a leader. She was very clever; she was very interested. Father was more of a reader and was a marvelous host in his own home. But he had no ability as a public speaker, though he had a good speaking voice, and he and Mother used a very good choice of words. But Mother could see right away that this was a new country and that she could be active in it. She enjoyed entertaining, and was a great worker in the church. She helped form the Women's Auxiliary, continuing there until she died, and worked with the IODE. She was remarkable for the times. She had no training for public speaking, but took charge of many meetings. The times needed someone that could take a leading part in things. There are some people that are leaders and some people that aren't.

❧ After I stopped teaching, in 1910, I always worked for the parish. I was always into something. I worked at something all the time because we needed that. You know, when you're starting a new place that's what's needed. When we left Michigan it was hard to leave our nice home; we didn't know what we were going to find. I wanted to have my education. Well, I sacrificed my education, but my everyday life was an education for me because I could do so much for the community. I can't now, but I've done my share. I was strong and healthy and I could do lots. I can't reproach myself for not having done what I should. It was all thanks to my dad and my mother. There was nothing they wouldn't do to help. They were more or less leaders.

❧ It was necessary for my husband's work that he have a chemistry laboratory. The CPR owned a building in Calgary that had been built up purposely as an office, but they never used it. They said we could go and live out there. We moved in; it was very comfortable, but within about two weeks the wind began to blow from the northwest, a nice gentle little breeze, bearing with it the most terrible odor you could imagine. I asked my neighbor about it. "This has been going on for months," she said. "It's so bad we can hardly stand it. We have gone around the area with a petition to City Council, to have them come out and investigate this odor. We know that it comes from the Burns Packing Plant." The plant had just burned down. Carcasses that had been hanging in the plant dropped down and had been lying there for weeks; smoldering for weeks and weeks. "That is the cause of the odor," said my neighbor, "but the city has done nothing about it. Our petition is there and we haven't even heard from them."

So the next day I went to town, to the city offices. The receptionist said that the mayor was in Council. I waited a few minutes and was ushered in when they had finished up their business. The mayor said, "There's a Mrs. Potter who wishes to say something to us." So I described the odor that we were being afflicted with in this part of town and told them that the petition had never been acted upon. The mayor spoke up: "I've never known there were any petitions." Pretty soon someone said, "Yes, we found those petitions."

They began to question me. One gentleman spoke up and said, "Oh, I don't think there's any odor out there enough to disturb anybody." I said, "You bring your wife out and spend one evening, and you'll change your mind. No person can stand that for any length of time." The others tittered about the way I'd called him down on that. They went on discussing what it could possibly be. I said, "There is no need for you to talk about where it comes from. It comes from the P. Burns Packing Plant." One of the men spoke up and said, "Well, how are we going to put that out?" I immediately spoke out, saying, "Doesn't the city own a fire department?" That, of course, raised another laugh.

The next day, in came the fire department and reporters from the Calgary paper and some of the City Council and they went to work. They worked there for a week, I guess, before they finally got that under control. I've often used that as an illustration of the times in a person's life when just asking or pleading or petitioning have no effect. It became necessary for somebody to take the bull by the horns. Then we got action. We drift because of a lack of leadership.

As women began to grow in the knowledge of their own leadership capacities, the beginning of World War One reminded them that there was a world beyond the frontier to which they must respond, no matter

how far it was. As single men left for training camps, women were aware of currents larger than "what we could see with our own eyes."

🕊 There were quite a lot of the boys went and some of them didn't come back. None of my own were in it; that makes a difference. I had no personal feelings about it. Like everyone else, I deplored it, of course, and we knew it was terrible. I did a lot of knitting; that's about all I could do.

Ann Wade's words were repeated in one form or another by many women. Knitting, sewing, and waving at trains defined their personal experience of the war. The knitting drew women together as they conversed over their work, getting better acquainted with each other. Their language, as they spoke of the war, was sympathetic, but rarely passionate; they were oddly detached. Margaret Furness, now in a nursing home at the end of a busy life, recalled with emotion her school friends who enlisted and died so long ago. "We felt that it was a terrible sacrifice for nothing in the end." Only Millie Melnyk, passionate and poetic, conveyed her memories of the war years with more intensity than most women. "The moon would be round, a full moon, and it would be red. Mother would stare at it and say, 'That's the blood of the soldiers overseas.'" Can it be that war was a male experience, perceived by women as remote and futile? Male leaders and writers thought of it as a watershed; in women's lives it was merely a moment. Most women who talked of their involvement spoke of it a lot less pompously than male politicians who ranted about "the sacrifices of our women for the war effort."

🕊 I sewed with the Junior IODE. We made those bandages. My brother, who was in the war, said they were cootie catchers; they just invited the cooties to snuggle in. The waste of material and labor ... I think we knitted belly bands too to wrap around their stomachs. They were useless. I suppose it wasn't a waste of labor because we were having a good time. Everybody would take their turn bringing down a cake, and we had tea.

🕊 Even the children in school knitted face cloths. God knows if the soldiers could ever use them. We were still in Calgary when war was first declared. The *Herald* put out a special edition and they went up and down the streets calling out, "Extra! Extra!" I wanted to see the boys go off to war. My mother and father and the neighbors went off to see Mrs. Mackintosh's two brothers go. No sooner were they out of the house than their daughter and I grabbed the milk money and got on the Red Line streetcar and got down to the station before the train went out. We left my two little brothers alone in the house; can you imagine doing a trick like that? Of course, we didn't want them to see us. We waved to the troop train and then had to rush like mad to get back on the streetcar.

🔥 I reported to the work room in Frank, and used to come down every Thursday. We walked down that three miles and I'd pick up a bundle of sewing and take it home and then bring it down with the next lot. I always devoted Friday to the Red Cross work. We made nurses' aprons and surgeons' gowns and knitted socks. Sugar was short then, and some things were rationed. A lot of things happened that didn't affect you personally, but you knew they were going on.

🔥 I can remember the ladies gathering right there at our house, sewing for the Red Cross. For the size of our population, there was quite a percentage of boys that went. What took them? Perhaps it was to get away. Some left families, though not many. One, Bobbie Johnson, went, and his wife stayed. But she was just as good as any man anyway to work at home.

The politicians solemnly pronounced that Albertan women would get the vote, previously denied them, as a reward for their contributions to the war effort. As women saw those sacrifices, ironically, so too did they see the suffrage. More often than not I heard, "I've forgotten what year it was that women got the vote. I didn't care very much one way or the other." If one hears only the leaders of the women's suffrage movement, one is led to imagine that the desire for suffrage was widespread. Perhaps it was, but much as I wanted to find evidence, the women I talked with did not provide it. It would take many more years for women to insist forcefully on the equality that must be theirs. Most of them were still reticent in 1916 about demanding the vote, citizenship, and equality, still reluctant to seize chances for power.

🔥 The women talked about having a vote and the men didn't think too much of it. But then they thought, "Well, it's a small country; there aren't too many voters, really, when you stop to think of it." It usually followed that the political thoughts of the husband were those of his wife. In one family that woman didn't agree. He said, "You have to vote the way I do." He told her that her vote would cancel his, and what would be the sense of it? You talked in your own family about your political thoughts, but women didn't talk much about politics when they were out.

Margaret Lewis, who organized a suffrage society and Women's Institute, Calgary, early 1900s.

Suffragists Nellie McClung and Emmeline Pankhurst, 1916.

❦ I had seen suffragists parading in London. When I came out here as a war bride, in 1918, the government gave a dinner at Government House for all the wives; then the Hudson's Bay gave us a luncheon and Nellie McClung spoke. She was all for the women. She gave a very good speech, and she said, "The main thing is to do what you have to do, but just don't become a drudge to your husband." A lot of the women agreed with her, but so many of the others had got used to being tramped on.

Indeed. Only a few of them were as outspoken as Amy Smith, who told me, "As soon as I knew that boys would grow up to have a vote and I wouldn't, I became a suffragist." Or Jehanne Casgrain, who observed, "After we women had the right to vote, then we voted. It was natural. It was normal." If not natural, women were beginning to learn that it could be normal.

❦ I remember one old lady at a convention. She gave a lecture as good as R.B. Bennett. She was dressed in an old shaggy sweater and she was telling about her experiences in Saskatchewan. She told us about sitting up at night knitting, and the things they were doing for the war effort. That's about the first time I heard a woman address a public gathering like that, because the notables in Calgary were all men. It wasn't the fashion. The women hadn't come to the fore then. They were minding their own business. And yet they were the ones that had to worry and make ends meet, and yet had nothing to say about it. If they expressed their views, they were just held down because they weren't supposed to know anything.

There was a lot of resentment. I think the feeling that was growing in women didn't come just overnight. It had been simmering for years. During the war, women were sent to munition factories, and helped out with the war effort. Then the men found out, and the women, too, that they could do other things besides keep house and raise a family.

Women began to gain the kinds of experiences that would eventually allow them to see full and unequivocal participation in the affairs of the world as normal. They first experienced political participation in women's organizations. The Women's Institute, the IODE, farm women's organizations, church societies, charitable associations, and groups with avowedly political purposes provided women with a forum for their early political energies. Many of the participants in these movements saw their activities there as appropriate extensions of their roles in the household, while others recognized that they were moving into another realm, the public sphere. Still others saw that they served to make their society more habitable, enhancing the lives of individuals by improving institutions such as hospitals and churches.

My mother was involved in the Women's Auxiliary of the church, and in the local Council of Women. The activity she was most involved with was the women's hospital group, because that's when the first hospital was being built in Calgary. There wasn't the money in those days, and you were always working to raise what you could. They supplied the linen and furnished the rooms, and that sort of thing. My brother and I between us raised enough money to buy a rocking chair for the hospital. Everybody helped that way.

I was in the Ladies' Aid for quite a long time. We used to meet twice a month and did some sewing. We had a bazaar once a year to get some money. We undertook to pay the organist at the church and to provide different things for the church. We bought an organ back in 1920. We just did things to make money for the church.

The National Council of Jewish Women had started here before I arrived. Their philosophy was education and social action. They were teaching immigrants. It was the kind of organization that appealed more to the affluent women. They're always called—what do they call them?—Lady Bountiful. I resent that name, you know. All it was was a woman who might know somebody who needed something, and who carefully protected the person it was going to. She'd say, "Don't ask; it's necessary," and would then pass on what was necessary very gently. So I always resented the name Lady Bountiful.

Individuals made attempts to provide services in a harsh country, but in the end groups had to organize to serve the huge number of needs ignored elsewhere. Irene Gilman recalled a "good neighbor lady" whom she loved more than her own relatives. When Gilman's husband had to go to Edmonton to the hospital there—bits of shrapnel were infecting his leg—this neighbor brought milk and butter for the children. "As far as the government was concerned, we could have starved to death; would have if it weren't for that woman." Individuals needed to become members of groups; the work of institutions needed to become more overtly political. The women recognized that together they would learn to organize, to speak in public, to run meetings, to lobby, and to participate in the world.

🔥 When I go down east on the train and see those elevators at the head of the lakes—the Alberta Wheat Pool, the Saskatchewan Pool, the Manitoba Pool, the United Grain Growers—I could just stand up and cheer. I feel so stirred by it. The farmers have managed to organize and have accomplished a great deal in that. They haven't abolished poverty, but they've improved their lot, and along the right principles of people working together and not trying to exploit each other.

My work with the United Farmers was a natural progression from the principles inculcated in me in my childhood. I had heard the farmers complaining about the treatment they got at the elevator companies on the matter of grades and dockage. There were an awful lot of interlocking directorates until the farmers woke up and organized the Alberta Wheat Pool; I'm very enthusiastic about it still, although no battle is ever won. Some of them were satisfied to be deprived; some people used to say that the farmers could never hang together. But they did manage to.

My involvement with them began in 1919. One of the first interests of the women's section was medical care. They were agitating for health care way back. The women would meet separately and draw up some resolutions, chiefly on health and education; they would bring them in and the men would almost automatically pass them. For many, many years they were asking for some sort of public health service, and the men backed them up.

🔥 A friend of Emmeline Pankhurst's, the English suffragist, came out here. She started the Alix Country Women's Club. From that, the United Farm Women started. It simply changed the life of the whole district because we got to know everybody. Without that, everybody would have kept very much to themselves. It brought them all together.

The Country Women's Club was invited with other women to come up to the United Farmers of Alberta convention by Mr. Woodbridge, the secretary. They went up and formed their own organization. The first year it was the Women's Auxiliary to the United Farmers. The next year, Mrs. Irene Parlby was provincial president. She said in no way were they going to be an auxiliary; that they would take care of their own organization and would not be just an arm of another. She spoke to Mr. Henry Wise Wood about this idea, and the women formed their own organization independently.

The sociability, the sense of working together, was what made the women so faithful. One Thursday a month was the day for meetings at Gleichen. At Alix it was always Saturday; everybody took the cream to the local creamery that day. There were various aspects of the farm women's movement. There was the desire to overcome the loneliness; there was the urge for companionship. It gave them something else to think about. It was perhaps the most educational influence that came to the west. The women learned to conduct their own meetings. They learned to develop their talents as executives.

❧ Sure, I used to go to United Farm Women. We learned how to run a meeting there. You remember old Aberhardt. I can remember this Sunday when he was preaching. He said, "The UFWA, now what's that? The UFWA? Oh, now I know! That's the United Fool Women of Alberta!" That was a good organization.

❧ The Women's Institute in Carmangay met twice a month. During the war they did work for the Red Cross, of course. They had gotten the Women's Institute started just about that time. In the little town, the women would come in from the country with a horse and a buggy. They'd come with their husbands. He might do his business and then go to the bar. Well, the women with the children had no place to go; no place to change their babies, warm their bottles, nurse them, and so on. So, the Women's Institute decided that they were going to do something about this. They first rented and then bought a little old building and fixed it up. They put in a stove and utensils so there would be places for the ladies to make a cup of tea or to warm something for the children to eat. There would be somewhere for the children to go to the toilet.

It became the place where the country women could go and visit. They needed conversation with the town women. It became the center of the women. The Women's Institute knew that the women in the country needed to learn how to cook and manage and that they also needed to know a bit of home nursing. There was a doctor in Carmangay, but to travel in a horse and buggy for a long way to take your child to a doctor wasn't instant service. So the Women's Institute together with the agriculture department of the government sent out a lady from Ontario.

She had a car equipped to show women how to cook. She gave recipes and directions for canning and so on. The car would stop in town for a whole day. The children and parents could inspect the display and get ideas. Then she helped form women's groups so that they could look after themselves in their own communities. That's how the Women's Institutes started in many other places. It filled such a great need. The women needed something. A woman can't live to herself alone.

Nor could a community take shape and develop if its people lived only for themselves. Women began more and more to participate in the kinds of activities that would build communities, bringing with them the lessons they had learned at home and in their new organizations. Not all of them, and not all of the time, but slowly, slowly, some women realized that their efforts could create a hospitable society. Their efforts would transcend the domestic sphere, move beyond desires for economic profit and individual gain, and engage with the public realm. Women would join together in fidelity to each other and to a future. The future they worked to create was one whose people were no longer isolated, but whose lives were bound together in a common world.

PHOTO CREDITS